HOME GUN
CARE & REPAIR

HoME

STACKPOLE BOOKS

GUN CARE & REPAIR

by
Parker O. Ackley

Harrisburg, Pennsylvania

HOME GUN CARE AND REPAIR
Copyright © 1969 by
THE STACKPOLE COMPANY

First printing, May 1969
Second printing, July 1969
Third printing, February 1974
Fourth printing, April 1975
Fifth printing, November 1976
Sixth printing, April 1978

Published by
STACKPOLE BOOKS
Cameron and Kelker Streets
Harrisburg, Pa. 17105

*Published simultaneously in Don Mills, Ontario, Canada
by Thomas Nelson & Sons, Ltd.*

ISBN: 0-8117-2028-4 (pap.)

Printed in the U.S.A.

Contents

Chapter

Chapter

Preface

This book collects not only what the owner should know about cleaning his guns, but it also contains information on how to do a variety of small maintenance and gun-improvement jobs that owners and sportsmen are frequently inclined to undertake. Necessarily this includes some small repairs. Whether or not these will happen to cover some specific gun model or problem encountered by the reader cannot, of course, be guaranteed, however experience has shown that of the various minor repairs described, counter-part procedures will often solve many though certainly not all of the somewhat similar problems encountered on guns other than those which happen to be mentioned in the text.

Yet this certainly is not intended to be any sort of gun-smithing book, a brand to which I would most strenuously object. The truth is that for several decades many gun owners have performed for themselves such small tasks as installing sling swivels and slings, recoil pads, and numerous varieties of sights, quite often including the telescopic ones. Certain new rifle barrels, already headspaced at the factory, can sometimes maybe be successfully installed by gun own-ers, themselves. Except for the Win. M94, the Marlin lever-actions, and some of the rimfire .22s, most guns requiring new barrels must be returned to the factory, however, for such jobs.

Gunsmiths do most of these different kinds of jobs, true enough, some often specializing, for example, in the installa-tion of 'scope mounts, ramp front sights, etc. How much of this sort of thing one wishes to label as gunsmithing is left to the reader, but as a rule the professional gunsmith is occupied mainly with far more complicated work, depend-ing on his equipment, the size of his shop, and the demand in his area or that which he has decided to cater to as a professional specialty.

There are instances when it may be necessary to return a gun to the factory for repair or "customizing." While Public Law 90-618, the Gun Control Act of 1968, prohibits unlicensed persons, with few exceptions, from buying, selling, or otherwise transferring rifles, shotguns, handguns or ammunition outside of their home States or in any form of interstate commerce, the legitimate owner of a firearm under Federal, State and local law may continue, of course, to mail his firearms to any licensed manufacturer or dealer for the desired repair or custom work. Since it can be furnished in many instances in advance, it is always well to write for a cost appraisal of the work thus gaining the opportunity to receive as well any special instructions that may apply.

The question of safety must be kept foremost in the minds of those who wish to tinker with guns at home. The question is a valid one—just how much and what kind of maintenance or repair should an owner try to tackle? Before trying to answer this, I think of a .22 rifle I once saw, its receiver and the rear of its barrel so often drilled and grooved by its owner in mounting various scopes and sights that it looked almost like a sieve! Had this been a high-power rifle developing some seventeen or more tons of breech pressure per square inch every time it was fired, quite possibly this shooter's gun tinkering would have long ago ceased. Yet as to the question of safety, here's where I think this book will help you for I've tried to include precautions wherever any critical areas are involved.

Mainly this book will interest those who already have some small tools including, let's say, a ¼-inch or larger (better) electric drill with maybe a few accessories extending its usefulness. Having made some small repairs, perhaps around the house, such a reader will have become familiar with the tools and be not altogether with resourcefulness.

If he breaks off a front sight just after the start of hunting season, he may be inclined to try to replace it himself rather than risk having his gun tied up too long in a repair shop. Or, having bought a new shotgun and finding its stock slightly too long to suit him, he may wish to reserve for himself the job of shortening it to fit, perhaps also adding a pad as part of the job. The extractor on his squirrel rifle may break or begin to cause trouble. Sometimes he will wish to install sling swivels on a deer rifle, new sights or perhaps a scope. Can he try to do such jobs by himself? Quite often he'll conclude, "Why not?"

Think always of safety considerations—first, last, and always—but don't hesitate to consult a gunsmith should you get stuck on some particular job started at home.

Aside from the engineering genius that goes into its design, a gun ends up as about six parts the result of skilled machining, about one part the result of metal-finishing skill in the bluing of barrel, receiver and small parts, and something like maybe three parts showing the combined skills of the carpenter and cabinet- or furniture-maker in shaping and finishing the stock. Consequently, if some new part must be machined—sometimes though not often the case—your gunsmith is likely best equipped to help you over the impasse.

Included in the book are some jobs that you probably may not feel up to in terms of skill or equipment, yet that's all right, too. Knowing in advance how a job is supposed to be done and what's involved is important—quite necessary to your decision as to whether you should tackle it or not. Then, too, this spares the grief, wasted time and effort arising when someone tries to do some gun tinkering at home that couldn't be done right by anyone without the right tools or equipment.

From several standpoints this book should help you derive the most pleasure and satisfaction in owning and caring for your guns. Also, if through its faults or disadvantages you've had to put aside some particular gun for a while, this book may help you overcome its handicaps and restore it to favor.

P.O.A.

CHAPTER 1

For Enjoyable
Gun Fixing—
Some Working Space and Tools

MANY SPORTSMEN already have a home workshop with some equipment suitable for work on guns. Others will have to start from scratch. But whatever the situation, the sportsman who wishes to work on his own guns need not put a strain on his pocketbook. He can purchase the few tools most necessary and add to them as the opportunity or need arises. Outstanding work is done by backwoods gunsmiths with no tools but two fifteen-cent files. However, when modern electric tools can be purchased at such low cost, it is unreasonable to use so much unnecessary elbow grease.

Looking at this chapter as a whole, the tools recommended may seem excessive. The tools listed here are enough for all the common phases of amateur gunsmithing, and no one is going to jump into the middle of all the different types of gunsmithing at once. Start your shop off with a good vise, a few good screwdrivers and a few good files. Add other tools as the need arises.

One of the best ways to learn about available tools is to get catalogs from a large number of suppliers. (See list in back of book.) The cost of these catalogs will run anywhere from a postage stamp to perhaps $3, but the information to be gained from them cannot be acquired from any other source for many times that amount.

Location

A home workshop can be located almost anywhere—such as in a vacant room, space in the basement, the attic, or space in some outbuilding. Often warm to work in during the cold months, the basement is especially desirable as most basements are fitted with drains which enable the worker to set up a small bluing outfit without the complications which would accompany it if it were set up in a room without sewer connections. However, a bluing outfit can be set up in a garage with a hose for water, if a place in the basement is not available. Proper ventilation can be secured with a fan and proper lighting with a fluorescent fixture.

Equipment

WORKBENCH   A workbench is a necessity. Highly satisfactory workbenches can be obtained from many suppliers, but it may be less expensive to build one from raw lumber or to convert a good *solid* old table for this use. It is desirable to have one or more drawers for the storing of tools.

A good way to keep track of your tools is to make a "toolboard" to set above the bench. Perhaps you have seen such a toolboard in a service station. On the board, paint an outline of the tool and place pins or hooks in the proper place to hold the tool over the outline. Then by glancing at the board, you can quickly see which tools are missing.

VISE   The most important single tool is a good vise—and by this is meant a *good* vise. About a four-inch swivel-base machinist's vise will suffice for all kinds of work including the making of stocks. It should be strong enough for all kinds of work such as removing some types of rifle and pistol barrels. Such a vise is relatively expensive and will cost from $30 to $50, yet there is nothing more worthless than a cheap vise. And under normal circumstances, a $10 vise is just so much money thrown away. Sometimes a good used vise can be found at a fraction of the cost of a new one.

Some vises have plain jaws which do not need changing. But most heavy vises have corrugated jaws—that is, there are teeth in them to keep the work from slipping. These corrugations should be removed, to prevent the guns from being marred. It is true that wood or copper jaws inside the jaws of the vise would protect the guns, but sometimes people get in a hurry and get careless, and if the protecting jaws are not available, they are tempted to say, "Just this once, it won't hurt," and thus a good gun may be ruined.

Since the vise jaws are detachable, being held in place by a couple of screws, they can be removed and taken to a machine shop where there is a large grinder (surface grinder is best) and the corrugations removed so that the jaws are smooth. Any machine shop will do this for a small price. When the jaws are replaced they will not mar the work nearly as much as if the corrugations were left on, and since there is no place for rough jaws in gun work, the vise is not damaged in any way. Before purchasing a vise it is well to check it over carefully to see what kind of jaws it has and purchase only one with detachable jaws which cover the entire surface, or jaws which protrude out somewhat from the casting, so that when the corrugations are ground off, thinning the jaws slightly, the vise will close tightly. It should again be emphasized that buying a cheap vise is false economy.

Special copper jaws can be made to slip over the jaws of

the vise. These copper jaws are finished from sheet copper, relatively thick—say ⅛ in., but any copper can be used. However, copper jaws are not adapted to holding small parts when they are being filed into shape. The hardened steel jaws hold small parts much more securely and accurately.

These copper jaws can sometimes be used to hold barrels being removed, but wood blocks sprinkled with powdered rosin are much more satisfactory for this purpose.

A set of wood jaws can be made out of plywood to fit any vise, and a set of such liners can be covered with felt for holding any part which might be damaged by holding it in an unprotected vise.

ELECTRIC DRILL   A ¼ in. (or preferably larger) electric drill is desirable. Some electric drill suppliers furnish complete kits containing all sorts of attachments fitting the drill. Some also supply the small stand which converts the small drill into a drill press, which is useful for installing sights, scope blocks and many other jobs not necessarily confined to the gunshop. A buffing attachment, which includes wire brushes and other attachments useful for buffing small parts and for stock work, are also available to fit the drill. Sears Roebuck, for example, features an exceptionally fine line of ¼ in. and larger drills; also for less than $12 they furnish a suitable stand to convert the drill into a drill press. A minimum set of drills can be obtained for $3 or $4. However, eventually the gun worker will want a complete set of wire gauge drills and a set of fractional drills running from 1/16 in. to ¼ in.

An excellent combination set of this sort is made by the Allenite Manufacturing Co., Chicago, Illinois. This is a 2,000 rpm, ⅜ in. electric drill, with an attachment to convert it into a drill press in a matter of one or two minutes. There is a sanding disc attachment which is fine for fitting a recoil pad. There is another small stand which can be bolted to the bench, converting the drill in a matter of seconds into a small electric grinder or buffer. This will also accept a fine circular wire brush. The set also contains attachments to convert the drill into an electric hand saw or bench saw with slightly over 1 in. depth capacity. In addition, there is a screwdriver attachment with a set of screwdriver blades, a few small drills, a socket wrench attachment, and other gadgets which are handy around the shop or the home.

In one of our local stores, this set was priced at around $30. I bought it to see if it would be satisfactory for use in a home gunshop and tried it out on many of the operations for which previously I had recommended the use of only an expensive drill press or lathe. And it worked! It worked very well! The chuck ran extremely true and I am convinced that this gadget is practical!

SCREWDRIVERS A variety of good quality screwdrivers is needed. It is necessary to have screwdrivers made from good quality steel, because soft metal will bend and mar screwheads. A great variety is necessary because guns have different types of screws and great care must be taken in loosening and tightening them to prevent damaging the heads. For example, in many fine foreign guns, the screws have been handfitted, are usually engraved, and always have a very narrow slot. To use an ordinary screwdriver on these is simply murder. The slots will be damaged and the appearance of the gun ruined. To keep from damaging these screws, it is usually necessary to grind the blades of several screwdrivers to the proper fit. Even if you are working only on American guns, it is necessary to have a wide variety, ranging from a complete set of jeweler-type screwdrivers all the way to the extremely long-shanked ones suitable for removing stock bolts.

If you need to buy a supply of screwdrivers, for less than $15, Brownell (see list of suppliers) can furnish an assortment of twenty-four screwdriver bits, each of which fits into one special handle. This set is of the best material and very strong, and the bits are properly ground for work on guns, and can easily be reground on a hand grinder.

Another good source of screwdrivers is Sears Roebuck, but be sure to specify "Craftsman" quality. All Craftsman quality tools are unconditionally guaranteed, and are replaced free of charge if they fail to give satisfaction. Another set of screwdrivers specially ground for gun work is the Grace set, selling eight screwdrivers for $8.

HAND GRINDER   While not a necessity, a hand grinder is a great convenience for work on guns. The Allenite set mentioned previously converts into a hand or bench grinder with one of its attachments, but it is too large to use as a hand grinder on guns. A very good hand grinder is the Dumore; another one is sold by Sears. Mounted points, grinding wheels and burrs are also available to fit these tools. This complete set will cost about $50.

TORCH   About the best torch for the amateur is the Prest-O-Lite kit which is relatively inexpensive and works off a small acetylene tank which can be bought or rented from any supply house at a relatively low cost. This one works exceptionally well for silver soldering. A very good torch of this type is also sold by the Johnson Gas Appliance Co. A less expensive torch, the Bernzamatic, which burns butane in a special small container, and the Turner Torch, which burns propane, also furnished in small disposable containers, are available in most department or hobby stores. These outfits, consisting of a gas unit, two sizes of burner tips and a lighter, sell for a very reasonable price.

Brownell lists a very good gas welding kit for less than $20. This torch uses butane and oxygen which are supplied in disposable containers. This will cost a little more but those who feel that they can afford it will find that they can do many jobs with it which otherwise would have to be taken to the welding shop. This welding outfit is not powerful enough to weld bolt handles, and these should be taken to a gunsmith. Before attempting any work involving heat on guns, read the section which follows on Safety. Any of these torches, of course, can be used to heat an old-fashioned copper soldering iron.

HAMMERS   A small and medium ballpeen hammer is necessary. A brass or plastic hammer is very useful.

FILES   Among the common tools in the gunshop, files are one of the most important and there is almost no limit to the variety that will be found useful. But to start with, you should have a complete set of needle files. Needle files are available from Brownell and other suppliers at 40c to 60c each, or $4.50 to $5.50 for a complete set of twelve. Many jobs can be done with a set of needle files which cannot even be attempted with standard files.

An assortment of flat and angle files with handles is desirable, but special files may be purchased as the necessity arises. For example, metal checkering files are extremely useful in checkering bolt knobs, the backstraps of pistols and revolvers, matting sights and ramps, and many other uses. For woodworking, you will need some woodworking files, but these need not be purchased until you need them.

HACKSAW   Another tool which is almost indispensable is a hacksaw. A cheap hacksaw frame is exasperating so only the best should be purchased and *only the best tungsten high-speed blades* will hold up for all kinds of gun work.

CLAMPS, PUNCHES, AND TAPS   For installing simple sights, the following tools are adequate: Parallel clamps such as Starrett #161C; a pair of inexpensive V-blocks such as Starrett #278; a set of drift or drive punches such as Starrett #565; a center punch; a cross test level such as Starrett #134; a few small taps for common screws such as 6-48 (a common size for attaching sight mounts); and taps for 6-32, 8-32, and 10-32 are desirable for miscellaneous jobs requiring these size screws. A supply of screws for use with these taps can be obtained from almost any hardware supply house.

This list of tools will be about all that is necessary, but they need not all be bought at once, but purchased as the need arises. And if you want to go farther, the catalogs of the gunsmith suppliers will furnish plenty of "wish" material.

Work Safety Considerations

There are common safety rules which anyone who handles guns should follow, but there are additional rules which every amateur gunsmith must consider every time he works on a gun. He must be certain that he has not *weakened* any part to a dangerous level. There are a few basic principles that he must keep in mind.

1. The judicious use of heat. Never heat the receiver ring of a bolt-action or any action which has its locking system within this area. Heat sufficient to melt soft solder is about the *maximum*. This means that such heat must be kept low enough so that the bluing of the parts or their discoloration will not occur. Silver soldering can safely be done on barrels or on the bridge of the action if care is taken to heat only enough to melt the solder. This temperature is somewhat below the original heat-treatment of the barrel and does no damage. On the other hand, if these are not evenly heated, or are heated to red heat, the barrel can become warped. When attaching a ramp to a barrel, using thin ribbon silver solder, care must be taken to heat the barrel all the way around, not just on top. Never silver solder on the parts of the receiver containing the locking system. Any time heat must be applied at any point near these parts, the parts should be wrapped in cloth, and the cloth kept wet to prevent the heat from creeping away and adversely affecting other areas.

2. Never remove excessive amounts of metal from points

of stress on the action. For example, it is dangerous to lighten a Mauser action by removing metal from the receiver ring. Some parts of an action can be lightened without a detrimental effect, but great care must be taken when working on critical parts.

3. Never use live ammunition when working on guns. Proper dummy ammunition should be made up and kept on hand for testing actions for feeding and other work requiring the use of a cartridge. These dummy cartridges can be made from fired cartridges by first re-sizing them, then seating bullets without repriming them or putting in the powder. Or, they may be made from new cartridges, by drilling a ⅛ in. hole in the side of a loaded cartridge, pouring out the powder and inserting oil in the case to kill the primer. Use caution.

If for some reason live ammunition is inserted in the chamber, the gun's firing mechanism should be removed or similar precaution taken to make it impossible for the round to be accidentally fired. But at all times, make sure that the muzzle is pointed in some direction where no damage would be caused in case of accidental discharge, even though the firing mechanism has been rendered inoperable.

4. Conversion of guns to handle cartridges other than the ones for which they were intended should be done only by competent gunsmiths. Some conversions are safe when properly done; others are on the borderline and leave no margin of safety; still others are definitely dangerous.

5. When fitting parts that must be made by hand or that come from the factory in rough condition and which must be altered for proper fit, make sure that these parts are functioning properly before actually shooting the gun, as improperly fitted parts can result in a dangerous condition.

6. In semi-automatic guns, when working on triggers to reduce the amount of pull, the arms should be tested with full loads (taking all precautions that no injury would result if such a gun went off accidentally). Set-triggers and other trigger

mechanisms which produce an extremely light pull should be tested before use by jarring the firearm to simulate the kind of quick jolt that might be experienced under actual use so as to make sure that the pull is not so light that the gun can be accidentally jarred off or discharged.

7. In the event of a hangfire when testing rifles, wait *a full minute* before opening the bolt. A great many accidents or blow-ups have occurred by opening the bolt too soon after a cartridge fails to fire.

8. Damascus barrels on old model shotguns are considered unsafe and should never be used for shooting modern ammunition.

9. A gun should not be held in the hands when test-firing. The gun should be held in some kind of a frame, the cheapest being made by tying the gun to an old automobile tire, and its trigger then being pulled by means of a string. Before test-firing, great care should be taken to make sure that the bore is clean and free from obstruction, and that the chamber is dry and not full of oil. When firing for proof-test for a rebarreled action, a factory cartridge lightly oiled is considered about the same as a blue-pill* test load since it is apt to develop considerable excess pressure when fired.

10. Never try to remove obstructions from a barrel by shooting them out. This practice will result in a swollen barrel with rimfire ammunition or a completely demolished barrel with high-pressure cartridges.

11. Before test-firing a rifle, make sure that the headspace is correct. This can be done in the following way, using factory cartridges. *Remove the extractor and the firing-pin mechanism from the bolt*, if it is a bolt-action, *or remove the mainspring or the firing pin* from other type guns. Then a live round can

*Blue-pill load—a cartridge loaded to yield pressure twice or several times that of the maximum standard load for that caliber. The idea is that if the gun does not blow up with a blue-pill load, it is unlikely to with the much lower-pressured standard loads.

be put in the chamber and the bolt closed on it. The bolt should close without any effort, meaning there is at least enough, or a presence of minimum adequate headspace. To determine next whether or not this headspace is *excessive* or too much, paper shims can be placed on the head of the case. Then close the bolt. This test can be repeated until sufficient shims have been progressively placed on the head of the case until the bolt will close only with difficulty. When this definite feel develops as the action is closed, the shims are next removed and their aggregate thickness measured with a micrometer. In a bolt-action, if the shims that can be placed on the head of the cartridge measure more than .005 in. or .006 in., the rifle may have *excess* headspace. This is nevertheless not an accurate measure since there is variation between different lots of factory ammunition. But such a test will show whether a rifle is safe or unsafe.

If there is a gunsmith close who has a set of headspace gauges for your caliber, by far the best idea is to *have him test the headspace.*

12. Never permit a cartridge in a gun in which the locking mechanism is faulty.

13. Never say, "Good enough," when working with guns. If you cannot say, "Right," put the gun in the antique cabinet or in the trash can.

14. Watch trigger pulls. Never make them so light that they are dangerous.

15. Always make sure that the gun is empty the minute you touch it, but always treat it as if it were loaded.

CHAPTER 2

Understanding
Rifles and
How They Work

SHOOTERS, when engaged in "gun talk" refer to the different types of rifles, and the different types are usually identified by their actions, the action being the main mechanism of the firearm to which the barrel is attached on the one end—the stock on the other. Actions can generally be classed as bolt-actions, tip-up actions, single-shot actions, lever actions, pump or trombone actions, and semi-automatic actions. These names are self-descriptive and each has certain specific advantages.

Types of Actions

TIP-UP ACTION The tip-up actions are similar to the single- and double-barrel shotguns, in which the breech tips up providing ejection of the cartridge and leaving the chamber open for the insertion of the new cartridge. These guns have been made in almost all sizes and designs. Both Savage and the Stevens Company have made a great many models of the tip-up rifle. Tip-up actions are usually unlocked by pivoting a small lever located near the hammer.

SINGLE-SHOT ACTIONS   Single-shot actions have been made in regular falling-block, rolling-block and drop-block versions. Among the best of the single-shot actions are the famous Winchester high and low sidewall. Another of the falling-block single-shot actions that is still much sought after is the Sharps-Borchardt. These actions are usually wanted for conversion to modern cartridges.

A number of .22 single-shots are patterned on the bolt-action design, some being independently cocked by operating the bolt or by pulling to the rear a knurled knob or ring at the rear of the bolt.

It is well to remember that in much of our American history single-shot rifles were the only kind available, and this usually put a premium on accuracy and good aim.

BOLT-ACTION   The bolt-action is so called because the action is operated by a bolt which locks the cartridge in the chamber and which has an operating handle or knob projecting at the side of the action. For repeating action, the bolt must be lifted and pulled to the rear, then pushed forward again and re-locked for each successive shot.

Bolt-actions can be further divided into (a) the regular Mauser system turning-bolt which requires the bolt to be raised and withdrawn, and (b) the straight-pull bolt where the bolt is simply withdrawn to the rear without first raising it (the turning being done by a mechanism within the bolt itself).

The Mauser-type bolt-action is the most widely used and the most frequently copied of all bolt-actions. The many variations of this type rifle include the 1903 Service rifle, usually referred to as the Springfield; and the 1917 Service rifle, usually referred to as the Enfield. The bolt-action rifle is extremely strong and most widely used for modern high-power cartridges.

How well the cartridge is supported in a locked, ready-to-fire bolt-action rifle is important. The better bolt-action rifles have bolts with an extra margin of strength since their bolt faces are sufficiently recessed to enclose part of the cartridge head when the rifle is ready to fire. Examples of such rifles are the Savage M110, the recent Winchester M70s, the Weatherby, the Model 700 Remington, and the Mauser M98. There are others.

Bolt-action rifles have one-piece stocks, which favor accuracy. Extraction of empty cartridge cases is also aided through the camming action occurring when the bolt is raised. Special models are available for southpaws.

LEVER-ACTION The lever-action is a typically American development, and until recent years has been the most popular type of repeating rifle. The 1873 Winchester was the lever-action made famous in early Western history, but the one that was and still is the most popular of all the lever-actions is the Winchester 1894, which is a back-locking lever-action rifle.

The Model 88 Winchester, on the other hand, is a front-locking type lever-action rifle, because the forward part of the bolt contains the locking lug, which is very like the straight-pull, bolt-action locking system. This type of action is less springy and just about as strong as the bolt-action. The Marlin system is just about the same as the Winchester except that while it is activated by a lever like the Winchester, it uses a slightly different locking lug, which allows the use of a solid-top receiver, incorporating side rather than top ejection as in the Winchester M94. This permits a scope to be mounted on top. The action is strong enough for modern cartridges like the .270 Winchester and the .30-06.

The Savage lever-action has always been a concealed-hammer or "hammerless" model with a solid breech. Position of

the hammer—cocked or uncocked—is determined by reference to a small projection at the top rear of the receiver.
Having a completely different cartridge magazine than other
lever-actions, the Savage M99 uses a spring-loaded rotary
spool magazine. It has proved a popular rifle for scope-mount-
ing.

PUMP OR TROMBONE ACTION   The pump-action has never
been as popular in the United States as either the bolt-action
or the lever-action repeater. It does give greater speed of fire;
it is the easiest action to work from the shoulder and permits
the shooter to recock and reload without removing his finger
from the trigger. However, the older models are not as rigid
and strong as the bolt-action and so are not chambered for our
most popular big-game cartridges, having been confined almost exclusively to those cartridges known as deer loads or
small-game loads. Because of the two-piece stock, which very
easily develops looseness, it is not generally as accurate as the
bolt-action. Often it does not have sufficient power to extract
and eject sticky cases. Also, its trigger-pull is creepy. But
because of its speed and lightness, it is used in many rimfire
rifles.

The Model 760 Remington is a modern pumpgun manufactured in the United States. It utilizes a turning-bolt locking
system similar to the Winchester Model 88. It has multiple-
lugs and is very strong. However, it does not have the camming power of the bolt-action. It is strong enough for modern
rimless cartridges like the .270 Winchester and the .30-06.
Nevertheless, it is much better adapted to handloading than
the older type pump-action.

Unlike the early Remington Models 14 and 141 which had
tubular magazines, the M760 is clip loaded.

SEMI-AUTOMATIC ACTIONS   The self-loading or semi-
automatic action is obviously the fastest of any system em-
ployed in non-military shooting. These guns are sometimes

referred to as "automatics" although strictly speaking, this terminology is incorrect. The automatic requires a single pull of the trigger to shoot all the cartridges in the magazine, whereas the semi-automatic requires a pull of the trigger for each shot.

An interesting semi-automatic is the Remington Model 8 marketed first in 1906 and designed by John Browning. This gun utilizes a turning-bolt system similar to that found in the Winchester Model 88, except that it is operated by recoil. It is relatively complicated, but very reliable and strong. Its later modernization was called the Model 81 Woodsmaster.

Most of the .22 rimfire semi-automatics are simple blow-back designs in which the gas force of the relatively low-powered .22 is offset by the weight and rear travel of the breech block, the action returned for reloading and readiness to fire again through spring action. For larger, more powerful cartridges, a different system is necessary. In 1905, Winchester brought out the Model 1905 Self-Loading for the .32 and .35 Self-Loading cartridges, employing a sliding weight in the forearm connected to the breech block to serve as a sort of "drag anchor" to handle the larger cartridges. Further Winchester improvements brought about the .351 Self-Loading model in 1907 and the .401 Self-Loading rifle of 1910.

Today's high-powered semi-automatic rifles are mainly gas-operated, bleeding off part of the cartridge gas to operate a piston and, in turn, the action. A spring returns the action again to reload and lock-up in readiness for the next shot. With this system the semi-automatic rifle can handle more powerful cartridges, the shooter enjoying at the same time less noticeable recoil—a side benefit of the gas-operated semi-automatic.

The latest self-loading rifles include the Model 740 Remington and the Model 100 Winchester. The M100 is essentially the Model 88 converted to semi-automatic gas operation by replacement of the lever with a gas piston, while the M740

Remington is merely the M760 Remington with a gas piston replacing the manually-operated slide.

Cartridge Nomenclature

The gun owner and especially the amateur collector of old guns is apt to become very confused by the various names applied to the many different cartridge calibers.

The older American method was to designate the calibers in decimals of an inch, with another figure designating the bullet weight. For example, in the case of the .45-70-500, the ".45" designated the actual bore diameter, the "70" designated a charge of 70 grains of black powder, and the "500" designated that a 500-grain bullet was used.

Some of these cartridges were also designated by simply using the caliber figure and adding some other identification such as .44 WCF, which translated, means "Winchester Center Fire."

Later, when more modern cartridges such as the .30-30 and the .30-40 were introduced, the first figure indicated the caliber and the second figure the weight of the smokeless powder charge. The .30-30 is sometimes designated as the .30 WCF, and the .30-40 is often called the .30 U.S. or the .30 Army because it was the official government cartridge first following the .45-70. Still later, the .30-06 took the place of the .30-40 as the government cartridge, the .30 indicating the caliber, and the 06 designating the year of its adoption.

Wildcat cartridges appear as soon as a new cartridge is introduced by one of the factories. Therefore, these have to have some kind of designation. For example, the .220 Winchester Swift was one of the first extremely high-velocity factory cartridges to be developed. Then wildcatters immediately started working over the Swift to some different form, often described as "improved." So the Improved .220 Swift, the .220 Arrow and many others came into being.

The Savage Arms Corporation introduced high-velocity cartridges such as the .250-3000, the name illustrating still another way to designate a cartridge—the .250 indicating the bore diameter and the 3000 indicating the velocity. Another of the .25 caliber cartridges is the .257 Roberts, where the .257 indicates the groove diameter and "Roberts" further identifies the cartridge. A .22-250 is simply the .250-3000 necked down to the .22 caliber.

European calibers are usually designated by metric measurement. For example the 7x57 has a bore diameter of approximately 7mm (.276 in.) with an overall case length of 57mm.

There are many other ways of indicating the calibers of cartridges, all of which adds to the confusion, and there is really no rule that can be used by the uninitiated. You just have to know or learn them.

Correct Headspace Is Important

With modern, high-powered cartridges, *excessive* headspace can be very dangerous. If your rifle has developed too much headspace, you must know how to recognize it so that you may take it to a gunsmith to have it corrected.

How well a particular cartridge fits the chamber of a rifle is frequently discussed in terms of headspace. To speak in broad generalities for a moment, no special headspace problems are usually encountered by the man who loads his rifle with the factory-made cartridges of correct caliber to match his gun. Furthermore, in the case of attempts to load a rifle where *insufficient headspace* is the problem, it is apt to be difficult, if not impossible, to insert the cartridge fully into the rifle's chamber and then completely close its action. Hence, when they arise, the majority of headspacing problems are of the kind where there is *too much headspace*. Still speaking in generalities, the shooter most apt to encounter this problem is the one who uses handloads now and then, rather than factory-made ammunition.

Most gunsmiths have gauges enabling them to check your gun and tell you the facts about the headspace in your rifle; this is by far your best resort for any questions relative safety, which loads you can use without worry, and so on.

Headspace can be defined in many ways. The common definition is as follows: Headspace is the space between the head of a fully-chambered cartridge and the face of a fully-locked bolt. This sounds very simple—and it would be, if all cartridges were of the same type. But we have four common classes of cartridge and headspace is measured in a different way for each type of cartridge. These four common classes of cartridges are: (1) rimless, (2) rimmed, (3) belted, and (4) rimless pistol cartridges.

DETERMINING HEADSPACE   (1) Determining headspace for the rimless cartridge. In a chamber for a rimless cartridge, the headspace is the distance between a fully-closed bolt (the head of the cartridge) and some point on the shoulder of the cartridge, referred to as its datum line (D in the Figure 1). The datum line is an imaginary line around the shoulder of the cartridge at a point where the shoulder measures a certain diameter. For example, the diameter of the datum line for a

Figure 1. (See Text re .30-06 and .270 Win. as exceptions.)

group of cartridges including the .30-06, the .270 Winchester, the .257 Roberts and the .244 Remington is .375 in., and datum line D is that imaginary line around the shoulder of the cartridge which measures exactly .375 in. in diameter.

(2) Determining headspace for a rimmed cartridge. In a rimmed cartridge, the headspace is determined by the thickness of the rim of the cartridge (Maximum and Minimum on

MAX.
MIN.

Figure 2.

MAX.
MIN.

Figure 3.

the diagram—Figure 2). This rim thickness varies somewhat, but a common measurement is .063 in. found in the .30-30 series of cartridges (.32 Special, .32-40, etc.).

(3) Determining headspace for a belted cartridge. In the belted cartridges, the so-called "belt" replaces the rim as described for the rimmed cartridges (Maximum and Minimum on the diagram—Figure 3). A common measurement is .220 in. for the .300 H&H Magnum, the .300 Winchester Magnum.

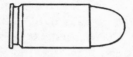

Figure 4.

(4) Determining the headspace of the rimless pistol cartridge. This type of cartridge, being perfectly straight and being rimless, has nothing such as rim, belt or shoulder to stop its forward travel as it is inserted into the chamber. In order to provide an accurate headspace adjustment, the mouth of the case is left perfectly square and comes in contact with the end of the chamber which is also square and abrupt, thus solidly holding the cartridge from moving forward. (See Figure 4.)

Certain tolerances are allowed in headspace measurements, usually referred to as "Maximum" and "Minimum." For example, a cartridge such as the .257 Roberts measuring from the face of the bolt to the .357 datum line is 1.7937 in. Usually the maximum, allowable headspace would be not over 1.7997 in.

The 7x57 (sometimes called the 7mm Mauser) is identical to the .257 except for the neck diameter, the .257 having been derived from the 7x57 simply by reducing the neck to .25 caliber. This means that the same headspace gauge may be used for the two cartridges. There are other cartridges which use identical headspace, a good example being the .243, .308 and the .358 Winchester, all three of which are the same except for the neck diameter, and all three use the same headspace gauge.

There is one exception to the standard datum line method of measuring headspace, and that is the .30-06 and its companion, the .270 Winchester. In the old days, headspace was measured from the face of the bolt to the top of the shoulder. This measurement for the .30-06 is 1.940 in. minimum and 1.946 in. maximum. The .270 Winchester is the same except for the neck specifications and is measured in the same way. The *modern* measurement for these two cartridges is 2.0479 in. minimum and 2.0539 in. for the maximum measurement to the .375 datum line. They both use the same headspace gauge. The data sheets for many currently manufactured cartridges omit measurements from the face of the bolt to the top of the shoulder entirely.

Summing up; headspace of most rimless cartridges is measured from the face of the bolt to the datum line. The only exception to the datum-line method of measuring headspace for rimless cartridges is the .30-06 and its companion, the .270 Winchester.

The official agency for determining final specifications for cartridges and chambers is Sporting Arms and Ammunition Manufacturers Institute (SAAMI), 250 East 43rd Street, New York. The official data sheet for any currently manufactured cartridge is $2 per copy.

Headspace tolerances for the rimmed cartridges usually are a little closer. For example, for the .30-30, the minimum is .063 in. and the maximum is .067 in. For the belted cartridge case, the tolerances are a little less; for the .300 Magnum, they are designated as .220 in. and .223 in.

Sometimes *excessive headspace* is indicated by an expansion in the case. However, before jumping to a conclusion that the chamber is oversize, the owner of the gun should measure the size of the unformed case—one never fired before—which may actually be undersize. If the chamber is oversize, it should be corrected.

Excessive headspace is often indicated by primer protrusion, which is merely a condition where the expended primer extends measureably from the head of the fired case. Primer protrusion is somewhat in proportion to the breech pressure

Primers protruding from fired cases, usually an indication of excessive headspace pressure in old rifles such as Marlin, Winchester and Savage. Excessive headspace pressure may result in cartridge separation, as in the case at the left.

when excessive headspace exists. If the strength of the brass case is sufficient to withstand the breech pressure, head separation is caused when the pressure developed inside the case is great enough to press the case firmly against the shoulder of the chamber and its head at the same time against the bolt.

Excessive headspace, however, is not the *only* cause of case separation. The forward flow of brass after repeated handloadings of rimless and belted cartridges often causes this separation. But, in general, if a case separation occurs, it is an indication of excessive headspace.

Often another cause of excessive-headspace problems is that the handloader fails to adjust his sizing dies properly.

Rifle Barrels

In order to more fully appreciate our rifles, we need to know a little about the barrels, the materials from which they are made, and the way they are made.

TWIST   All early barrels were smoothbore, but someone, believed to have been a German, discovered that spiral grooves inside the barrel would impart a spinning motion to the bullet and keep it moving more in a straight line. This idea was brought to America by gunsmiths who became settlers in the Pennsylvania Dutch country and here they developed the Kentucky Rifle, known all over the world for its remarkable accuracy.

The twist, sometimes referred to as the pitch of rifling, appears as a spiral on the inside of the barrel when you look through the bore of the gun. The rate of this spiral or twist depends on the length of the bullet for which the barrel is desired. A round ball requires little twist, sometimes as slow as one turn in 60 in., but the longer the bullet, the faster the twist required to impart a high rate of spin to keep the bullet head-on as it flies through the air. For example, the 200-grain

6.5mm bullet requires a very fast twist—something like one turn in 5½ in. or 6 in. The more conventional rifle barrel such as those made for the more popular modern cartridges usually perform best with a 10 in. twist. So-called "standard" twists have been determined for most calibers being manufactured. For example, for the .22 L.R., the standard twist is 16 in., while for the high-velocity center-fire .22 caliber cartridges like the .22/250, the standard twist is 14 in. The standard twist for the .30 caliber is one turn in 10 in., but some barrels are made 1-in-12 in. when it is known that the lighter weight bullet will be used.

STEEL   The most common type of barrel steel for high-powered rifles is chrome moly or, more accurately, chrome molybdenum (S.A.E. 4140 or 4140 modified). This is used because of its high combination of high-tensile strength, high degree of machinability and long-wearing quality.

Drilling and reaming methods have remained about the same for a long time. A solid bar of steel is drilled by a common deep-hole or gun drill, which is a single-lip drill capable of drilling a relatively straight hole in a relatively short time. This hole is then reamed to proper bore diameter by a special reaming machine using a series of three or more reamers. The finished hole is reamed to perfect size and is ready for rifling.

RIFLING   There are numerous methods of rifling the barrels. Some custom barrelmakers still stick to the original cutting method, which is done by means of rifling heads containing suitable cutters. But most large producers have changed to either the button method or the hammer method.

The button method can best be described as swedging and is accomplished by either pushing or pulling through the barrel a carbide button which looks much like a bullet that has been fired. These buttons are made of extremely hard tungsten carbide and have grooves ground into them on a spiral corresponding to the twist desired in the barrel. The grooves ground into the button, with the lands upraised are pressed into the steel, producing uniform lands and grooves in the barrel, with a resulting high finish impossible to obtain by the cutting method.

The hammer method requires a very specialized machine using a mandrel over which the rifling is produced. The barrel is actually hammered down on this mandrel by means of a special machine. This method also leaves a very perfect or high finish, but has not proved very satisfactory for the custom gunsmith because of high-cost machines and because this method has not produced the desired accuracy in the barrel. Button rifle barrels have demonstrated accuracy superior to all others.

A multigroove system was developed under pressure of times creating a need for lower-cost production. It has not proved successful and is rapidly disappearing. However, some modern advertising would have you believe that a tremendously revolutionary rifling method has been discovered which gives unbelievable results. In fact, this method was used a hundred years or more ago in some European barrels, especially sub-caliber and air-rifle barrels.

CHAPTER 3

Tinkering with Bolt or Lever-Action Rifles

INSTRUCTION folders for popular model rifles can be obtained from the factories free of charge. These contain breakdown and assembly data much better than can be given in this brief book. It is a good idea to secure these leaflets for the guns in which you are interested. Look up the addresses in the list of suppliers.

For those who can afford it, there is an excellent book for the assembly and disassembly of many obsolete guns. This is *The Encyclopedia of Modern Guns* by Bob Brownell, and is available from Brownell's Incorporated. (See list of suppliers.) This book contains illustrations of all the important parts for most rifles, shotguns and pistols.

The repair of many of these old guns is made difficult by the fact that the companies which made the guns, have discontinued the sale of all parts. A few companies manufacture parts for these old guns and some companies have made a business of junking old guns to make the used parts available.

Making Round Firing-Pins

One repair often needed on old guns is the replacement of the firing-pin. If an electric drill, such as the Allenite kit is available, many types of firing-pins can be filed out.

A good amount of padding should be used in the vise to hold the drill firmly in a horizontal position and a piece of metal—suitable material for the new pin and of proper diameter can be placed in the chuck. Then the tip of the firing-pin can be filed out by using round and other suitable files. It is necessary to leave a generous fillet (radius or taper) between the body of the pin and the tip. A square corner at this point will result instead in breakage. Some types of firing-pin require almost a square corner, but as much of a radius as possible should be left. If these parts are made out of drill rod, they can be left unheat-treated. However, if heat-treating is desired for the tip, it can be heated to a red color and quenched in oil, then polished and tempered when it again reaches a dark-straw or light-blue color. It is then again quenched.

The flats and notches in various types firing-pins can be filed out after the tip has been made as described above. The locations of the notches and flats are important and should be made as much like the old parts as possible.

Removing Dents From Tubular Magazines

A very common trouble in tubular-magazine type rifles is failure of all the cartridges to feed out of the magazine. This is usually caused by dents in the magazine tube. The dents can be raised by peening with a small hammer somewhat in the same manner as removing dents in an automobile. The best thing to use is a drill rod which may be obtained from any large hardware supply house, in diameters which will just slip through the various magazine tube sizes. These rods are three feet long, long enough to work through any magazine tube with a little to spare, and they can be kept for this specific purpose. However a rod as short as 4 in. or 5 in. may be used. The rod is forced into the tube to a position directly under the dent. The dent can then be raised by peening with a small hammer. When the dents are raised as much as possible, the job can be tested by simply dropping the magazine follower through the tube. It should drop through freely.

Corroded Chambers

One of the most common extraction failures in all kinds of .22 rifles is a scarred or corroded chamber. This is often caused by the excessive use of .22 Short ammunition. This causes a corroded ring right at the end of the .22 Short case. Then when a .22 L.R. is fired, the case will swell into this ring, making it impossible to remove the case. This requires either a new barrel or that the chamber be bushed. Either of these jobs is beyond the ability of an amateur, and should be taken to a gunsmith.

Removing Rifle or Pistol Barrels

The best way to remove a rifle or pistol barrel is to secure a piece of hardwood 1½ in. to 2 in. by 3 in. to 4 in.; 1½ in. by 3 in. works very well for most barrels. Using an ordinary brace and bit, bore a hole about the size of the barrel in the center of the block through its thin side. Then saw the block in two to produce two half-blocks with half a hole in each. The blocks will be used in holding the barrel tightly between the vise jaws, so the barrel can't turn.

For a different size barrel you will need a different set of blocks as the grooves must closely fit the barrel. Sprinkle powder rosin in these grooves and place blocks and barrel in the vise.

A large Crescent wrench or a monkey wrench makes a very good barrel wrench, especially if something such as a tough shipping tag is used between the wrench jaws and the barrel. Actually, you unscrew the receiver from the barrel when you turn.

Removing barrel from bolt-action receiver by using wooden blocks in heavy vise. Note the use of a shipping tag in the jaws of the wrench to protect the barrel.

This method is adequate to remove almost any barrel such as the Model 94 Winchester, the Springfield, the Model 70 Winchester or similar actions.

When removing most bolt-action barrels with a Crescent or a monkey wrench, the wrench is fitted tightly to the action just back of the recoil lug, with a piece of copper sheet or some other soft metal, between the top of the receiver and the jaws of the wrench. A large percentage of bolt-action rifle barrels can be removed in this manner. The Enfield is ordinarily very tight and requires both a barrel wrench and a barrel vise.

Actions such as the Jap, the Remington M721 and M700,

and a few military actions that do not have a flat on the bottom
of the receiver are best removed with an inside wrench, and
the removal of such barrels is beyond the capabilities of most
home workshops. It should also be mentioned that some barrels are so tight in their corresponding threads in the receiver,
that when they are finally turned, the surfaces of the threads
gall or freeze together before the barrel has been completely
removed, making it impossible to remove the barrel without
ruining the threads in the receiver.

Most rifle actions have a right-hand thread, but there are
a few that have a left-hand thread, for example, the Norwegian Krag and some models of the Ross rifle.

Repairing Bolt-Action Rifles

Bolt-action rifles normally require less repair than other types.
However, there are a few simple things that happen and which
can be repaired by the amateur in his home workshop. Most
of the bolt-action rifles are based on the Mauser. So while
reference is made to certain guns by name and number, most
of the repairs here described are applicable to many other of
the bolt-actions.

EXAMPLE—SPRINGFIELD RIFLE   The correct nomenclature
of the rifle known as the "U.S. Springfield" is "U.S. Rifle
Model 1903-A3, caliber .30." There are several variations of
this model with only minor differences.

The most common repairs needed on these models are on
the extractor and the ejector. The ejector is a small part which
fits into the recess in the left side of the receiver under the
bridge. It is held in place by a pin which has a split head. The
split in the head of this pin allows the head to be expanded
enough so that when it is pushed or driven into place, the
expanded head creates enough friction to hold the ejector in
place. The ejector simply pivots, or hinges around this pin.

The ejector itself is made in such a way that when the bolt is withdrawn to the rearmost position, the point of the ejector is cammed inward so that it passes through the split locking lug and contacts the rim or head of the cartridge which is being held in position by the extractor on the right side of the bolt. When the point of the ejector strikes the cartridge head, the cartridge is pivoted around the extractor and thus is thrown out of the gun.

When the 1903 rifle is disassembled, the ejector pin often falls out, resulting in the loss of the pin and ejector. Also the ejector may break so that it becomes inoperable. It is then necessary to replace the ejector. And, if the pin has a tendency to drop out, it can be held in a vise and a small screwdriver used to spread the head of the pin enough to make it friction tight.

The extractor is held in place by a collar which fits around the bolt. This collar has a dovetail that fits into a slot on the underside of the extractor. To remove the extractor, turn it around to the bottom of the bolt and slide it forward; or the hook of the extractor can be raised with a screwdriver to disengage it from the retaining slot on the end of the bolt, which allows the extractor to be pushed forward and off.

Springfield extractors have a way of getting loose. This is usually caused by loss of tension toward the rear end of the extractor, which is actually a spring. Sometimes the two ends of the extractor become bent enough to allow the extractor to become loose. If this occurs, a new extractor collar can be fitted, or sometimes the end of the collar can be bent down slightly by using a small hammer. If the extractor spring has become weak, the part can be bridged across the vise and a small ballpeen hammer used to put a little more bend in the extractor to create greater tension.

The firing-pin assembly of the 1903 rifle consists of three parts plus the mainspring. These parts are known as the striker (the tip end of the assembly—the part that actually contacts the primer), the firing-pin collar and the cocking rod or cocking piece. The striker has a recess milled into its rear end which fits into a dovetail arrangement on the front end of the cocking rod; the collar slides over this joint, thus holding these two pieces together. The mainspring fits around the cocking rod and pushes the firing-pin collar forward and holds it in place. This is one of the greatest weaknesses of the Model 1903 action because the dovetailed piece on the rear end of the striker sometimes breaks off allowing the cocking piece to come out of the bolt assembly. If this breakage happens to be caused by a blown primer or a blown cartridge head, the cocking piece is sometimes blown back with sufficient force to injure the shooter seriously. Under normal conditions, this does not occur. But for shooters who have a tendency to hot-rod their handloads, it is well to have a competent gunsmith fit a one-piece firing-pin or fit a so-called "safe" conversion. This simply consists of a small horseshoe-shaped piece which most any gunsmith with proper equipment can make and install.

Some 1903 rifle owners wish to have the cocking knob removed to create a faster locking time; in other words, a modified speedlock conversion. Usually this part is quite hard and must be annealed. This is best done by wrapping the sear, which is an integral part of the cocking knob, with a piece of wet cloth or wet asbestos, and slowly heating the knob until the shade becomes dark black or a very dull red. Sometimes the sear can be held in the vise, which latter will bleed enough heat away to prevent the softening of this part while the knob itself is being annealed.

After it is cool, the knob can be sawed off with a hacksaw and the end smoothed over with a file. The end can then be welded over to prevent the remainder of the knob from unscrewing, or, instead of welding, a small hole about ¼ in. or 3/32 in. in diameter can be drilled through the cocking piece and firing-pin so that a pin can be driven tight between the two pieces, then dressed off on both sides. This will prevent the cocking piece from unscrewing.

Sometimes the Model 1903 jams because the magazine follower becomes worn enough to allow one or more cartridges to pop up out of the magazine when the bolt is withdrawn with a snap. Usually this condition can be corrected by installing a new magazine follower.

Another common trouble with this model is the magazine floorplate falling out. This is caused by the magazine floorplate catch becoming rough or the spring becoming broken. This condition can usually be repaired by sharpening up the end of the catch or the lug on the floorplate which the catch engages. Sometimes a new magazine catch is required.

The old Model 1903 rifle often develops excessive headspace. These rifles with serial numbers under 800,000 sometimes have poor breechbolts. This is usually indicated by a small semi-circular cut or indentation on the back side of the left-hand, or split locking lug. This indentation sometimes becomes relatively deep and is caused by the bolt being slammed back against the cutoff. This occasionally becomes so bad that the bolt will come all the way out of the receiver after the cutoff has become cut all the way through the lug. It is advisable to have a late-issue bolt fitted to any of these old 1903 rifles having serial numbers under 800,000, even though the bolt does not show this indentation.

The magazine cutoff also acts as the bolt stop. It is a wing-shaped part on the left side of the action near the rear end. It is marked "on" and "off." When the wing is up, the word "on" appears; when the wing is down, the word "off" appears. When the cutoff is down, on "off", it prevents the bolt from coming far enough to the rear to pick up a cartridge from the magazine or to allow the bolt to catch on the rear end of the magazine follower. This arrangement was obviously put on this model to facilitate performance of the Manual of Arms. When the cutoff is in its up position, or "on", the bolt can be withdrawn far enough so that the magazine follower will pop up in front of the bolt, thus preventing the bolt from being closed without first pressing the magazine follower. For sporting use, the magazine cutoff should be left in the "on" position.

The cutoff is held in place by the ejector pin. To remove the cutoff, the ejector pin must be driven out, then the cutoff spindle can be withdrawn by means of a small screwdriver. The screwdriver can be inserted in the small groove cut around the spindle which protrudes slightly from the rear of the receiver.

EXAMPLE—MAUSER RIFLE   There are a number of models of the Mauser action. But the Model 98 is the best and the most common, and it is probably the best bolt-action ever produced from an overall standpoint. The more modern versions of the Mauser include the M1889 Belgium, the M1891, M93, M94, M95, M96, M1903, and M1924 and many others. The later models beginning with the M98 will have a third or safety lug which locks into the recess in the bottom of the receiver directly under the receiver bridge. The Model 1903 Springfield also has a safety lug, but instead of locking into a recess in the bottom of the receiver, it turns down just forward of the receiver bridge, thus creating a safety lug.

The bolt stop consists of a hinged "box" attached to the rear end of the receiver on the left side. This assembly includes the ejector as well as the bolt stop. The ejector seldom breaks, but sometimes it becomes too short. This condition can be repaired by removing the ejector, heating it and drawing it out by peening it with a light hammer. This will lengthen the part sufficiently to make for positive ejection of the fired cartridge case. Care must be taken to make sure the ejector is perfectly straight before it is replaced in the action.

The bolt-stop spring consists of a flat spring with a dovetail arrangement with two flat sections. One is the bolt-stop spring and the smaller one is the ejector spring. When the ejector spring breaks, it is necessary to replace it. Parts for the FN action interchange with the Model 98, which means that in the absence of military parts, a new part can be obtained from FN (Firearms International Corporation).

A common fault of the World War I Mauser actions is lack of hardness in the receiver ring section which contains the locking recess. Sometimes these surfaces are so soft that the locking lugs of the bolt "set back," thus increasing headspace. Sometimes the recesses inside the receiver ring become upset enough so that the bolt binds and can be closed only with difficulty. When this occurs, the throat of the receiver through which the bolt passes when it is closed, can be filed out slightly to remove these expanded or upset places, allowing the bolt to work freely again. But when this occurs, usually it means that the action has developed excessive headspace, which must be adjusted by turning the barrel in sufficiently to minimize the headspace. Receivers in this condition should be re-heat treated before reassembling them. This work must be done by a gunsmith with proper equipment, gauges, etc.

Almost all military bolt-actions have double-stage, and what is usually described as a "lousy" trigger-pull. The best way to do away with this fault is to install one of the patented trigger mechanisms such as the Timney, Canjar, Mashburn or Dayton-Traister trigger kits. (See list of suppliers.)

EXAMPLE—ENFIELD RIFLE   The 1917 Enfield is also a Mauser-type action but it does not have the same lug arrangement as described for the Springfield and Mauser 98. Instead, the bolt handle drops into a recess in the rear end of the receiver, which allows the bolt handle itself to act as a safety lug.

The 1917 Enfield has an extractor similar to the other two types. It is stronger than the Springfield, but not as strong as the M98, but the repairs are the same as described for the 1903 Springfield. The magazine floorplate is very similar to that of the Springfield and requires the same kind of repairs.

The most frequently encountered problem with the Enfield actions is the ejector breaking. The ejector is somewhat similar to the M98, but the original ejector and ejector spring were made in one piece. When the Enfield ejector breaks, it is best to replace it with the type that uses a coil spring. This type of Enfield ejector is available from Christy Gun Works. Once the amateur gunsmith has had a chance to examine one of these broken ejectors, it will be easy to see how to correct it. Even putting in a short loose piece of bent clock spring works.

Commercial bolt-actions have about the same kinds of weaknesses as military versions. The old type Winchester Model 70 for example, has the Mauser-type extractor. But the ejector was somewhat improved and seldom causes any trouble. The Remington models, especially the 721 and 722, develop both extractor and ejector problems. There appears to be just no way to repair these extractors. The only repair is replacement of the part. The later Model 700 Remington and similar ones, has a somewhat improved extractor arrangement. But here again, the only repair is part replacement. The ejector on these models and some other commercial actions consists of a spring-loaded plunger installed in the face of the bolt. This causes no trouble unless a cartridge case-head is badly blown. Then sometimes the ejector is forced back into the bolt and cannot be removed at all. But usually when this occurs, the head of the bolt is expanded, thus rendering the bolt completely useless anyway. When a bolt has to be replaced, it is necessary to return the complete rifle to the factory.

Repairing Lever-Action Rifles

Again, it should be pointed out, that although definite model numbers of guns have been used in this book, this does not mean that the repairs apply only to these particular guns. If you will carefully examine your gun, watching to see just how the parts work, you will see many similarities to the repairs described and you can apply these repairs to ones needed in many other makes and models.

EXAMPLES—TYPICAL WINCHESTERS   The Model 94 Winchester is essentially the same as the two late models, namely the M55 and the M64, which means that most repair jobs for one are common to the others. There are several troubles that they share in common.

1. Failure of the cartridge to feed out of the magazine, caused by dents in the magazine. This can be repaired as described in the previous chapter.

The magazine tube can be removed by first removing the screw holding the plug in the muzzle-end of the tube, being careful not to allow the plug to fly out and become lost, as the magazine spring is often strong enough to make this plug fly many feet unless it is carefully held while being removed.

If the gun is a carbine model, the magazine is further held by the upper and lower magazine bands through which screws extend, holding the magazine tube in place. When these two screws are removed, the tube can be slid out through the magazine bands.

If the gun is a rifle, the magazine tube is sometimes partially held in place by means of the screw holding the magazine plug in place and also by a pin through the ring surrounding the magazine tube. Using a small drift punch, drive out this pin. Then pull the magazine tube forward to a point where it is free from the forearm tip. Never attempt to drive out *the magazine ring.* When the magazine tube is free of the forearm tip, twist it around from left to right. This will turn the magazine in its recess, which is actually a semicircular recess rather than a dovetail. The dent can then be removed as described in the previous chapter.

When replacing the ring, care must be taken to get it in perfect position before turning it into place. Otherwise the recess will be damaged. Often these rings are driven out by someone who believes that it is a simple dovetail, and when this is done, the semicircular recess is ruined and the ring is damaged to the extent that it is almost impossible to ever again make it do its work, and often it has to be soft-soldered in place in order to make it stay there permanently.

2. Jamming. A loose cartridge guide, especially the one on the left side, often causes a stoppage. This is a tricky condition to diagnose. Often the Model 94 Winchester will thoroughly jam when being operated from the shoulder, because the shooter naturally cants the rifle while operating the action from the shoulder. This allows the loose cartridge guide to protrude into the action thus preventing the cartridge from coming up through the cartridge guides as the shooter attempts to feed the next cartridge into the chamber. When the rifle is taken down from the shoulder and operated in a horizontal position, it is also natural for the shooter to cant the rifle the other way, which reverses the condition. Yet, in case of a loose left-hand guide, the rifle will function perfectly when it is held in an upright position.

The repair is simply to tighten the screw holding the loose guide in place. For the left-hand guide, it is necessary to remove the spring-cover, often referred to as the loading gate. Then a small screwdriver can be used to tighten the cartridge-guide screw. This requires a small offset screwdriver. One suitable for this job is impossible to purchase, therefore it has to be made. A screwdriver with a shank of about 3/16 in. diameter can be heated and bent to the proper shape and then retempered. To retemper a tool of this kind, heat the end for about ½ in. or so, to a cherry red, and quench in oil or water —preferably oil since this has a tendency to make the metal slightly less hard than does water. Then polish the business end by using a piece of emery cloth or by touching it on a grinding wheel. Then slowly reheat it until the color changes to a dark-straw or light-blue color, at which time quickly requench it. If the resulting tool is too brittle and breaks, the whole operation must be repeated and the tool rehardened and redrawn, heating to a darker color such as a dark blue.

3. Ejection of more than one cartridge at a time. Failure of a cartridge stop to work allows a loaded cartridge to come out of the magazine either under or over the cartridge carrier. This thoroughly stops things and when it occurs, it is necessary to remove the link. This is a plate hinged at the forward end of the receiver, the lever working at the other end. This plate closes the bottom of the receiver. It does not have to be removed completely to get the cartridge out from under the carrier. Simply remove the holding screw in the forward end of the link and push out the hinge-pin. This will allow the front end of the link to drop down, allowing the loaded cartridge to come with it. To completely remove the link, it is necessary to remove the lever. This is done by first completely closing the action. By observing the right-hand side of the receiver, it will be noted that there is a hole near the front topside with no screw in it. On the other side of the receiver, directly opposite this hole, there is a screw, which is simply a dummy screw. Remove this screw and then, using a small drift punch from the right side of the receiver, drive out the lever-pin through the left side of the receiver. The lever will come out of the gun with the link attached to it.

The cartridge stop is a small projection at the forward end of the link. The reason that it allows a loaded cartridge to pop out of the magazine under the carrier, is because the end is worn or damaged enough to fail to hold the next cartridge in the magazine. Often this condition can be rectified by holding the small projection on the flat surface of a vise and drawing it out slightly by peening it with a small hammer. Actually this requires only a few thousandths-inch change so often the peening idea works out very nicely. If the cartridge stop cannot be drawn out enough in this manner, then it can be built up by silver-soldering on a small piece of steel and then dressing it down to the required height.

4. Failure to open. A very discouraging type of stoppage in the M94 is caused by the ejector pin working out and

catching along the side of the receiver. Sometimes when this occurs, the lever can be moved very little or not at all, making it seem as though the action is completely frozen.

The trouble can be diagnosed by removing the hinge-pin holding the link, thus allowing the link to drop down to the front, which will enable the ejector-pin to be observed from the lower side. If it has worked loose, it can sometimes be pushed back into position by using a screwdriver. Once the pin is pushed back into position far enough to allow the action to be opened, it is necessary to remove the breechblock in order to make permanent repair. This is done by first removing the lever as described above, then removing the hammer and hammer-spring, which in turn will allow the lower tang to be pushed to the rear and out of the receiver. Then remove the carrier. This will allow the breechblock to come completely out of the action, which makes it possible to peen the ejector-pin tightly into place.

5. Failure to eject the fired cartridge caused by a broken ejector. The ejector is a small bar-like part protruding from the lower front edge of the breechblock. The ejector stop pin holds the ejector in place, working through a slot in the ejector. Sometimes the part breaks, allowing the forward portion of the ejector, which actually kicks the fired cartridge out of the action, to fall out and become lost. It is easy to ascertain if the ejector is broken or not by examining the front end of the breechblock when the action is open. When the action is open, the ejector extends out from the bottom of the breechblock. If there is simply a hole or slot visible, then the front end of the ejector has broken off and fallen into the action. It is easily replaced, but requires a new part.

6. Failure to fire. This is usually due to a broken firing-pin. Breakage usually occurs at the very tip-end. If the firing-pin tip is broken off, a new pin is required and may be made as described at the beginning of this chapter.

If misfiring is caused by a badly-worn action causing so

much headspace that the firing-pin will not reach the primer, the only repair that can be made is to adjust the headspace. This usually requires that the barrel be set back one thread and rechambered, and this can be done only by a gunsmith who is properly equipped. When the barrel is set back, it is necessary to refit the forearm and magazine tube by shortening them an equal amount.

7. Failure to extract. This may be caused by a broken extractor. It is not necessary to disassemble the rifle to replace the extractor. Simply open the action all the way, which will expose the pin holding the extractor in place. The pin can be driven out by using the proper size drift punch and the new part installed. In case a new part is not available, one can be filed out, but a good grade of steel should be used. One of the best materials to use for this kind of work is ground flat stock. Brownell lists an assortment of flat annealed spring stock which can be used for making small parts that need to be heat treated. Small parts can be made out of ordinary hot-rolled or cold-rolled stock which can sometimes be found in salvage yards, or can be obtained from supply houses carrying steel. Old-time gunsmiths sometimes used old spring leaves from buggies and similar material for making parts.

One of the easiest ways to file out a part of this kind is to soft-solder the original part which is used as a pattern, on top of a piece of flat stock. Then shape the new part with saw and file, exactly like the pattern, but allow enough extra material to replace what was worn off. Then simply separate the two pieces by use of a torch. By using this type of material, it is unnecessary to heat-treat or temper the part. If heat treatment becomes necessary, it can be brought to a red heat and quenched in oil or water. Most steel used for these parts is water-hardened, but if the parts are thin or slim, oil-hardening is preferred. Then the parts should be tempered by heating them as evenly as possible, yet quite slowly, to a light-blue color and quenching them in oil. The part should be soft enough so that it can be cut with a file. If it is so hard that it cannot be filed, it will be so brittle that it will break too easily. Hardening and tempering techniques for parts of this kind vary greatly with the type of steel. The above procedure is based on material such as flat stock, drill rod, Starrett Ground Stock or ordinary spring steel.

Failure to extract can also be caused by badly-scarred chambers which make it necessary to knock out the fired cartridge with a rod. If a chamber is scarred or corroded, an examination of the fired case will show the trouble. This is a condition which cannot be remedied except by a fully-equipped gunsmith.

The lever may become dented or nicked enough to prevent the extractor from moving freely in its slot. If this is the case, the extractor will not snap down over the rim of the case, thus leaving the fired case in the chamber. Such a condition can be remedied by removing the extractor and then removing dirt or nicks from the breechblock by using a small needle file. When the extractor is replaced, make sure that it is free by moving its forward end up and down, making sure that it snaps into the lowest position freely.

Sometimes the lever becomes difficult to operate, so that it becomes stuck when one tries to open the action. This is caused by the friction stud being rusted, or the friction stud spring being too strong. The friction stud is a small plunger protruding from the rear end of the link, which snaps into a small recess in the lower tang. This stud and spring are held in place by a small crosspin. To remove, drive out the pin and pull out the link. If the parts are rusted, the hole should be cleaned out and the rust removed. Then all the old parts should be oiled and replaced. If the spring is too strong, remove one coil at a time until the stud works freely. Sometimes the wedge-shaped edge of the stud may require smoothing before reassembly.

8. Failure of cartridge to feed into the chamber, either

striking the top or bottom as it tries to enter the chamber. This is caused by a bent carrier, sometimes referred to as a cartridge-lifter. If the carrier is bent up it will raise the bullet end of the cartridge too high, causing it to hit the top of the barrel instead of entering the chamber. This condition is easily rectified by removing the carrier which is held in place by two screws, one on either side of the receiver. The bent carrier can then be easily straightened and replaced.

If the carrier is not coming up high enough, it may be because the notch at its rear end is so worn that the carrier spring, held inside the receiver by a screw, cannot hold the carrier in its topmost position. This requires replacement of the carrier. If you can't find another one, it is necessary to repair the old carrier, a job for a competent gunsmith.

But, if the carrier appears to be in good condition, the same trouble may be caused by a carrier spring, and repairing this trouble will cure the problem. This spring can easily be removed by first removing the spring cover which then exposes the screw holding the carrier spring in place.

The carrier of the Model 94 is a little tricky to install. Hold the gun by the barrel with the top of the receiver upward. Holding the carrier by the front portion, insert it—rear end up—in the receiver, flat side toward the rear, and align the screw holes in the carrier with those in the receiver on both sides, making sure that the screws will enter the carrier without damaging it by bending it. Then seat the screws firmly. Now swing the carrier forward and up into the receiver. Make sure that it functions freely.

A malfunction that is common to many of the tubular-magazine rifles like the Model 94 and the Marlins is caused by the magazine tube coming loose thus permitting it to move forward enough for the rim of a cartridge to catch in the space between the bottom end of the magazine tube and the receiver. This is more common with the Winchester because its magazine tube is held in place by a pin through the magazine ring engaging in a semicircular cut in the magazine tube. This semicircular groove is sometimes damaged when the retaining pin is driven in with the magazine tube not properly positioned and its groove not lined up with the corresponding one in the ring. It is sometimes difficult to repair a magazine tube which becomes thus deformed. In this case, however, the magazine tube can be shortened ¼ in. at the end entering the receiver, which will permit the tube to move forward through the ring, thus offering a new place for a retaining cut to be made. This semicircular cut can be made with a small needle file. Some gunsmiths make this cut by using a drill which closely fits the hole in the ring, but when doing this, make sure that the tube does not turn or move while drilling is done.

CHAPTER 4

Pumpgun and Semi-automatic Rifle Problems

IN THE FOLLOWING pages difficulties pertaining to specific rifles are considered. Most pump rifles, of course, are .22 caliber. While your rifle may be of some other make than those referred to here, quite possibly the needed repair can be handled in one of the ways discussed. Before any repair work is undertaken, it is necessary to establish the exact cause of trouble, of course. Usually this can be established simply through careful inspection or examination, or you may know already what the trouble is.

Repairing Pump Rifles

TYPICAL WINCHESTERS   The Winchester Models 90, 06 and 62 are very similar, being .22-caliber pump-action rifles. These are very durable models and when one can be found in good condition, it is a very desirable firearm. There are not many stoppages that cause trouble in these models; those that do are easily repaired.

1. Broken carrier spring. The carrier or cartridge-lifter has a small spring attached to the top and one side of the carrier. It is held in place by a small screw. This is a very small, thin, flat spring which can easily be made out of a piece of clock spring of about the same thickness. Spring material such as this can easily be drilled if care is taken not to force the drill too rapidly. A good lubricant to use is ordinary nitro solvent such as Hoppes #9. Put the spring material on a piece of hard wood to support it while it is being drilled. Once the hole is made, the spring can be filed to proper shape and bent fairly easily without breaking it, if reasonable care is taken.

2. Jamming. Another cause of jamming in these models is the carrier itself becoming bent so it prevents the loaded cartridge from fully entering the carrier. If this occurs, all that is necessary is to bend the upper prong of the carrier out sufficiently to allow the cartridge to drop in freely.

3. Failure to fire and extract is not too common in these models, but sometimes the firing-pin or the extractor can become broken and require replacement. Parts are so difficult to find that, unless they can be secured from dealers in surplus or used parts, they may have to be repaired. This is best done by a competent gunsmith.

TYPICAL REMINGTONS   The Remington Model 12 was one of the all-time popular .22 rifles. It was introduced in 1909 and discontinued in 1936, but it was continued after 1936 as the Model 121, which is merely an improved Model 12. Since the M12 and its successor, the M121, are highly-desirable models exhibiting much finer workmanship and much higher-quality materials than many of the current models, there is substantial demand for these rifles in good condition.

There are numerous things which cause jams and stoppages in the Models 12 and 121.

1. Failure to release when fired. Sometimes the cartridge carrier will not rise high enough to release the action after it is fired, so that the action cannot be opened without unlocking it manually. This can usually be remedied by slightly bending down the middle of the mainspring rod, where it engages with the rear of the carrier.

2. Failure to lock. Sometimes the action fails to lock—the opposite of the above situation. One reason for this may be that the front-end of the carrier does not go down far enough to engage properly with the carrier-dog. To remedy this, remove the carrier and from its front, cut away some metal where it rests at the front end of the guard. Do this very gradually, so as not to cut away too much.

Sometimes the carrier is operating perfectly, but it fails to lock the action when fully closed. This can be due to a rounded or worn corner which engages the carrier dog. If it is not in too bad condition, it can sometimes be squared up by grinding it enough to again create a square corner. However, in many cases the cure requires a new carrier.

3. Failure of carrier to lift cartridges. If the carrier fails to lift the cartridge when the action is moved forward, the carrier-dog spring may be weak or broken. This requires replacement of the carrier-dog spring. A new spring may easily be made from one of the springs found in one of the excellent assortments such as those sold by Brownell. If the carrier-dog is broken, a new part can be made by anyone who has available the use of a small lathe.

4. Cartridge striking the edge of the chamber. One of the most common stoppages experienced with the M12 is the cartridge striking the edge of the chamber as it moves forward into the chamber. This is sometimes caused by dirt under the extractor which prevents the extractor from going far enough down to hold the cartridge in correct alignment with the chamber. To remedy this, simply clean away the dirt from under the extractor.

Another possible cause may be wear on the extractor itself, which allows too much space between the extractor hook and the breechblock.

This trouble also might be caused by the extractor spring becoming jammed with dirt or becoming rusty. The spring should be replaced if rusty. Since this is a coil spring, again Brownell's spring assortment may have to be put to use.

5. Failure to extract. The extractor often becomes faulty. The main cause of this is that the extractor hook may become dull or the extractor spring weak. Usually the extractor hook can be sharpened with a small file or the extractor spring may be replaced from the spring assortment. W.C. Wolff Company, is another supplier of springs of all kinds (see list of suppliers) —recoil springs, hammer springs, firing-pin springs, etc., for rifles, shotguns, and pistols. These are furnished either singly or in kit form.

Sometimes a burr in the edge of the chamber causes extraction failure in the M12 and many other makes and models. The burr is caused by dry-firing the rifle, or snapping it while empty. This small burr can sometimes be removed by using a round needle file. Sometimes this notching damage will be deep enough to cause the cartridge to rupture when the gun is fired. A deep notch is caused by too much snapping on a long firing pin. The only remedy for this damage is to replace the barrel or bush the chamber, either of which jobs must be done by a competent gunsmith.

6. Failure to feed. Sometimes a cartridge fails to feed from the action bar up into the breechblock. Sometimes this is caused by excessive wear and can only be cured by replacement of the breechblock. In this case, with new parts not available, the only source for a new one is one of the dealers in used parts.

7. Failure to fire. Misfires are most commonly caused by a broken firing-pin. The older M12 firing-pin is of the flat type and is relatively hard to make. But there are several companies

who now manufacture this kind of firing-pin—The Christy Gun works and Numrich Arms Company can furnish at least some of the parts for the M12.

Another cause of misfires is the one described previously wherein a deep notch has been developed in the chamber by dry-firing. When the burr around the notch is removed, a depression still remains, thus leaving no support for the rim of the cartridge right at the point where the firing-pin strikes it. The only way to remedy this is to replace the barrel or bush the chamber, something to be done only by a gunsmith.

Misfires in all kinds of .22s are often caused by the breaking or the wearing of the mainspring. When this happens a new mainspring is required.

The Model 14 Remington is a pump-action rifle, and the Model 141 is the improved model of this same rifle. The M14 was an extremely well-made gun, but was quite complicated and this resulted in a number of definite troubles.

1. Extraction failures. These may be due to a broken extractor, a weak extractor spring, a dull extractor hook or a damaged chamber.

If the chamber is rough, sometimes it can be polished enough by a piece of emery cloth wound around a split rod, with the whole placed in the chuck of an electric drill. Insert this polishing rod into the chamber to polish out a burr or roughness.

If the extractor hook is dull and slipping off the cartridge rim, it can be reshaped by using a small file to increase the bevel of the hook and at the same time, to sharpen it a little.

If the extractor is broken, a new part is required. A new extractor spring can be made from one of the spring assortments mentioned before.

2. Failure to eject the empty case may also be due to a weak extractor or a broken extractor spring and can be repaired as described above.

It can also be caused by a broken ejector rod. This is simply a straight rod with a notch in it. A new one can be made out of a piece of drill rod of the proper size.

3. Failure to feed. The M141 gives less feeding troubles than the older M14, but both develop the same troubles. Like the M12, dirt may accumulate under the extractor, which will prevent the extractor from holding the cartridge in perfect alignment. A weak extractor spring may cause the same trouble. Both of these troubles are corrected in the same way as that condition in the M12 Remington previously discussed.

The other main cause of failure to feed into the chamber is a carrier dog which is too short. This fails to raise the carrier high enough to properly align the cartridge with the chamber. In the absence of a new part, the old carrier dog may be lengthened slightly by heating and peening.

Sometimes the cartridges will not feed from the magazine into the action bar. This may be caused by the follower sticking in the magazine tube. In this model the magazine has a spiral groove pressed into it for the purpose of preventing the round-nosed bullets from detonating a next forward cartridge in the magazine. If the follower sticks in the tube, it may be caused by dirt in the dents and this must be removed. Then check to see if the follower will drop through the magazine freely.

This failure to feed from the magazine into the action bar may be caused by a weak magazine spring. If so, a new magazine spring is needed.

One of the most serious stoppages is the failure of the cartridge to feed from the action bar into the breechblock. There are a couple of notches on top of the action bar which line up with slots in the breechblock. As these parts wear, the action bar will move a little too far forward as the action is closed, resulting in misalignment between the breechblock and the action bar. The remedy for this is to bend the magazine tube to throw the action bar upward, which will result in a closer fit between the rear end of the action bar and the breechblock.

Another possible cause of this trouble is a carrier lever that is a little too short. To correct, the carrier lever must be replaced or lengthened.

Sometimes the magazine follower comes too far back into the action bar. This is caused by the loading bar and the action-bar cover getting out of adjustment. The remedy for this is to bend the middle of the cover downward to prevent the follower from coming so far back.

4. Misfires. Misfires may be caused by a weak mainspring or a broken firing-pin. Since parts for the M14 are extremely hard to find, anything done to remedy the situation must be done in the shop. Close study of the trouble will usually reveal the exact cause and then the necessary repair must be figured out by the mechanic himself.

Maintenance—Semi-Automatic Rifles

REMINGTONS AND BROWNINGS   The Model 24 Remington is a self-loading .22 rifle designed by John Browning and introduced in 1922. It was discontinued in 1935, but was reintroduced as the Model 241 in 1948, manufactured for a few years, and then permanently discontinued. A few years ago, the Browning Arms Co. reintroduced it as the Browning .22 Automatic Rifle. The currently manufactured rifle is similar to, although not identical with the M241 Automatic.

All three of these rifles are of the take-down type. The take-down is accomplished by simply unlocking the barrel and unscrewing the interrupted threads from the receiver. The Model 24 requires a half-turn to remove the barrel since it has two sections, and the two later models require a one-third turn since they have three sections in the barrel.

Because of this removable barrel feature, very poor accuracy is realized with sights or scopes mounted on the receiver, because the barrel will move as it warms up, thus changing the bullet's point of impact. This merely means that all scopes and sights must be mounted on the barrel, and not wholly or partly on the receiver. There are several special scope mounts designed particularly for the Browning, which install on the barrel and extend back of the receiver. These mounts will work also on the two Remington models. Ejection is accomplished through the bottom of the action and this sometimes gives rise to problems of interference between an empty case trying to get out and a fresh case trying to get in.

All these models have take-down adjustments. The adjustment ring is a threaded ring screwed onto the barrel threads to form a sort of locknut between the barrel and the receiver. When the barrel becomes loose, it can be tightened by revolving the adjustment ring until the barrel can be screwed into its proper position, though this can be done only by some effort.

There are numerous causes of stoppages in these models.

1. Failure to close. Sometimes the action fails to close. This may be caused by powder residue accumulating inside the action, although it can also be caused by rust. The remedy for this is to clean the action thoroughly and oil it lightly with light lubricating oil. Excessive fouling of the action due to powder residue is common to most of the autoloading .22s. The model which is most reliable and less susceptible to this sort of fouling is the Model 03 Winchester, which was later modified and called the Model 63.

Sometimes the cartridge will not quite enter the chamber because it contacts the cartridge guide. This is caused by the cartridge guide becoming fouled with dirt or powder residue. The simple remedy is to polish the bullet incline.

Sometimes the action will not close because the magazine tube is fouled with powder residue. Sometimes the cartridge will stick in the tube due to dents. The magazine tube for these models is located in the buttstock. The tube must be thoroughly cleaned and dents removed as described at the beginning of this chapter.

Sometimes the cartridge guide-spring is out of adjustment. Clean and adjust the cartridge guide-spring. If this does not remedy the trouble, a new spring may be necessary.

2. Failure to open. Sometimes the action will not open all the way or not enough to eject the fired case and allow a fresh cartridge into the barrel. This is often caused by an excessive amount of powder residue inside the action which prevents the breechblock from traveling all the way back. To remedy this, simply give the action a thorough cleaning.

All semi-automatic rifles of the simple blowback type sometimes develop an eroded chamber. Usually this can be corrected by polishing the chamber with a piece of emery cloth wound around a split rod, which is then placed in the chuck of a drill. If the erosion is too deep, the chamber can be bushed, but this must be done by a competent gunsmith. Rusting in the chamber may be treated in the same way.

Excessive chamber corrosion is caused by the breechblock opening while powder is still burning in the discharged cartridge case. There is no remedy for this since this is one of the blowback system's principles of operation.

3. Failure to extract. Extraction often gives trouble in these models. The extractor is a dovetailed part which slips into the breechblock from below and is held in place by a detent pin* and spring. Sometimes this pin and spring will get out of position, making the extractor inoperative. If the spring and pin are only out of position, they can be cleaned and put back in operation. If the part is lost, a replacement will have to be found though this is sometimes hard to do. Try Christy, Numrich, and Wolff for parts. (See list of suppliers.)

*A pin having on its side a small indentation, or special cavity by means of which it can be held in place, as by means of a spring-loaded plunger.

4. Rifle fails to fire. If the rifle fails to fire, the same old powder-residue accumulation may be the cause. If so, the action must be thoroughly cleaned.

The firing-pin may be broken and require replacement. This is usually beyond the capability of an amateur and the problem should be taken to a gunsmith.

The mainspring in these guns is a coil spring which fits inside the firing-pin. It sometimes becomes too weak to fire the cartridge, in which case the mainspring must be replaced.

5. Rifle fires more than once with each pull of the trigger. The sear notch may be broken or worn. This usually requires a replacement of the sear. Sometimes the sear notch can be sharpened by using a small hand hone. These parts are usually too hard to be cut with a file.

The repeat firing may be caused by a worn firing-pin notch and if this is the case, a new firing pin must be provided.

CHAPTER 5

Shotguns
and How
They Work

A DISCUSSION of shortguns seems to make use of a variety of rather confusing terms. One may say, "My favorite shotgun is a 20-gauge double-barreled Ansley H. Fox, with an improved-cylinder right and a modified left." To the uninitiated it means nothing.

Shotgun Gauge

The gauge of a shotgun is the size of the bore of the barrel. The gauge was originally named for the number of bore-sized balls of lead that it took to weigh a pound. That is, ten lead balls the diameter of the bore of a ten-gauge shotgun weighed a pound, while it took twelve of the twelve-gauge balls, or twenty of the twenty-gauge balls to weigh a pound. The smallest size shotgun is .410, but this is not really a gauge but a caliber, and .410 is the actual size of its bore. However, these round balls have nothing to do with the modern shotgun, as

shotgun shells of today are loaded with pellets running from
BB-size to #12-size shot.

Choke

A shotgun barrel is smoothbore, having no rifling, and is
constricted at the muzzle-end to concentrate the pattern of
shot. This constriction is called "choke." Degree of choke
refers to the percentage of the charge which falls within a 30
in. circle at a distance of 40 yards. If a barrel makes between
70% and 80% of the shot fall within a 30 in. circle, it is called
a Full-Choke barrel; between 65% and 70% equals Improved-
Modified; 55%-65%, Modified or Half-Choke; 50%-55%,
Quarter-Choke; 45%-50%, Improved-Cylinder; 40%, true or
straight Cylinder. This applies equally for all sizes of barrels;
that is, the size of the pattern is the same for all gauges,
8-gauge to .410, the difference otherwise being in the number
of shot in the charge and the number of shot represented by
the various percentages.

Shot Patterns

You can easily pattern a shotgun by setting up a piece of paper
about eight-feet square. Then measure off 40 yards and shoot
at this target paper. Then draw a 30 in. circle to include the
densest part of the pattern and count the number of shot holes
inside this circle. From the following chart, the number of
shot in the shell used may be learned.

Shot Size No.	Pellets per Oz.	Shot Size No.	Pellets per Oz.
BB	50	7½	350
2	88	8	409
4	136	9	585
5	172	10	868
6	223	11	1,380
7	299	12	2,385

Note: It is worth patterning your shotgun because a barrel identified as Modified Choke will probably now give virtually a Full Choke
pattern with the recently developed plastic shells and their improved
components.

Assuming that #6 shot is being used in a 20-gauge gun, a common shot charge is one ounce, which means that the entire charge contains 223 pellets. By counting the number of holes inside the 30 in. circle, it is easy to compute the percentage of shot which struck inside the circle. This will give an indication of the choke in the barrel. It may not be an absolutely true indication as some barrels will handle certain sizes of shot more efficiently than others. The best way to determine the choke is to pattern the barrel several times with each size of shot.

Shell Designations

Shotgun chambers and shotgun shells are designated by the length of the chamber and the length of the shell. The standard 12-gauge shell is 2¾ in. *after* it has been fired. Twelve-gauge shells are also available in 2½ in. and 3 in. sizes, the 3 in. being designated as "Magnum" and such a shell, of course, requires a 3 in. chamber. Shorter shells can be used in the 3 in. chamber, but it is *dangerous* to try to use the long shells in a chamber which is too short.

Types of Shotguns

Shotguns may be divided into five types: Single-barrel (single-shot); Bolt-action single-shot, bolt-action repeaters; Double-barrel (which are further divided into side-by-side and Over/Under); Pump or slide-action; and Semi-Automatic, which are further divided into recoil-operated and gas-operated. A few lever-action repeating shotguns were manufactured years ago, but they never achieved popularity.

SINGLE-BARREL SHOTGUN   This is the simplest type of shotgun and usually the cheapest. Both older and some current single-barreled guns represent the tip-up type, a kind that shoots one shot and breaks open (the rear of the barrel tipping up) to reload. These guns, almost exclusively, use the under-bolt locking system which is simple and strong, a system activated by moving a top lever. This type is exemplified by the ever-popular Iver Johnson Champion and by any number of similar guns manufactured by the Stevens Arms Company, the Harrington & Richardson Company and the Hopkins and Allen Company. For many years these guns, all of similar design, were sold at low prices. They were essentially good guns although many thousands were retailed at less than $10 apiece. Many of these guns can still be picked up. Parts for them are pretty rare so for any necessary repairs the parts often must be made by hand. For the amateur gunsmith, they offer a tempting field.

BOLT-ACTION SINGLE-SHOT SHOTGUNS   As stated above, the older single-barrel shotguns were almost exclusively of the tip-up type, but as price competition entered the picture, even lower-priced bolt-action shotguns were introduced. This type of gun was invariably of cheap design and construction and is best described as crude. They are subject to many troubles and, with the possible exception of mail-order houses, no parts are available. If you already have such a gun, think in terms of making necessary repairs by hand.

DOUBLE-BARREL SHOTGUNS   Double-barrel shotguns come in two types—side-by-side—where two barrels are placed one beside the other—and the Over/Under, where one barrel is placed above the other.

The side-by-side double-shotgun has been the most popu-lar shotgun made, at least until a few years ago when the pump and the automatic achieved their present popularity. How-ever, the double-barrel shotgun is far from dead. Many are imported into the United States, mainly because the cost of production of a good double-barrel gun, with all its necessary hand-fitting, is prohibitive in the U.S.A.

Most double-barrel shotguns are the tip-up, break-open

type, actuated by a top lever similar to the top lever used on a single-shot shotgun. Some have two triggers—one for each barrel; others have a selective-single-trigger that gives the shooter the choice of firing either barrel first.

In the years prior to World War II, some of the finest shotguns in the world were manufactured in the United States. Among these were the famous A.H. Fox, the Parker, the L.C. Smith, the Ithaca, and the Lefever. Since these guns, to many, are irreplaceable, their value is increasing by the minute. Even the Field-Grade guns, which originally cost only about $50, if in good condition will now bring two or three times the original cost, while some of the Special grades bring $2,000 or more. This probably shows that there are still people in the United States who appreciate the fine workmanship that was found only in these guns, which were all hand-fitted and were actually works of art.

The earlier models of these famous makes were made with either twist or Damascus barrels, which are discriminated against as they are felt to be unsafe with modern powders. But they are still beautiful guns, and if you wish to use them today, there are several companies that specialize in fitting steel barrels to these fine old actions. Among them are Armaf, Westley-Richards and Atlas Arms. Also some of the better old-time shotgun actions can be fitted with a set of rifle barrels. Frederic F. Breitwiser specializes in this work. (See list of suppliers).

Amateur gunsmiths can often pick up these old double-barrel shotguns in good condition except for a broken stock, a broken spring or a broken firing-pin. As a spare-time project these guns may be restocked and refinished so that they will again become useful guns or good trading stock.

Many thousands of double-barrel shotguns were sold to the American shooting public under trade names. Many of these guns are still in existence but most are practically worthless. Many are so loose that they are unsafe. All are impossible to repair unless all parts are made by hand or secured from companies which specialize in parts for these old guns. Numrich and Martin Retting are two of these. If you send them a complete description of the gun, these companies are often able to provide serviceable used parts.

Aside from having the finest workmanship, which now seems like a lost art, double-barrel guns do have certain advantages. They are the safest of all guns. By merely breaking them open, you can see at a glance whether or not they are loaded. Also, it is easy to look quickly through the empty barrels for barrel obstructions, a feature convenient to all shooters, especially handloaders. With the same barrel length, you can get a gun several inches shorter than the pump or automatic. But the greatest advantage is that the owner has at his instant command two different degrees of choke. The standard combination of the double-barrel shotgun is the left barrel full choke, and the right barrel modified choke. However, different combinations are available.

Over/Under double-barrel shotguns provide two degrees of choke, the same way as the side-by-side gun, the main difference being that the one barrel is above the other. This introduces certain problems to which the side-by-side is not subject. In order to extract the fired shell from the lower barrel, it is necessary for the Over/Under to break through a much larger arc than is necessary for the side-by-side.

Another objection to the Over/Under is the unequal recoil from the different alignment of each barrel in relation to the shooter's shoulder.

Many shooters of the Over/Under claim that a great advantage is the single sighting plane—that is, the shooter looks over one barrel instead of two. This probably is mostly imagination, because whoever saw a side-by-side gun with more than one sighting plane—the rib right down the center of the barrel? Another point in favor of the side-by-side is that the Over/Under usually costs more for a gun of the same quality.

The single-barrel gun can be recompensed for its lack of different degrees of choke by installing some type of choke device. These are generally of two types—a variable-choke, which allows the degree of choke to be changed by means of a graduated collar or cone; or a group of interchangeable choke tubes which can be carried by the shooter and changed for different types of shooting. These devices increase the versatility of the single-barrel gun.

It is more difficult to make a stock for an Over/Under than for a side-by-side. But for either, an amateur who has patience and aptitude can shape a stock which will result in a gun that fits him better, and shotgun fit is one of the prime requirements for success with a shotgun. If proper fit and choke is obtained, the shooter can practically disregard the gun. If it does not fit, he has to take a bead on his target and it can get out of range before he can fire the gun. (See text on "Making Your Stock Fit You," chapter 14.)

PUMP OR SLIDE-ACTION SHOTGUNS   Pump-action shotguns and semi-automatic shotguns are inherently of such design that fine workmanship cannot be incorporated except for a fancy stock, beautiful engraving, etc. Actually they are "sloppy mechanisms" which means that they are noisy and occasionally unreliable. Being single-barreled, they have only one degree of choke unless they are fitted with some type of choke device. But many of the adjustable-choke devices produce very satisfactory patterns.

The pumpgun has been on the market for many years. The first really successful pumpgun was the 1897 Winchester. This old gun has probably the strongest action of any pump shotgun ever produced. It was noisy, and usually the hunter in the next field could tell when one of these guns went into action, because the gun would go "Boom-Clatter-Clatter; Boom-Clatter-Clatter" and so on, the noise of the action making almost as much noise as the explosion of the shell! But the action always worked. It was well-built and would last a lifetime under the hardest usage. This was proved from the use by our Armed Forces of thousands of these guns known as "trench guns" and "riot guns." They were very much reminiscent of the Model T Ford. When one stopped working, all you had to do was pour in a handful of parts and start over again.

Many of these famous old guns, although no parts are available, are rapidly increasing in value. A good Model 97 or Model 12 will command a price several times the original cost. The only salvation from a spare-parts standpoint, is that some small manufacturers are now making fair-quality parts for several of the famous old models. For example, several companies manufacture spring covers (loading gates) for the 92 Winchester rifle, firing-pins for the Model 12 Winchester, and similar often-needed parts for other makes and models. Also some companies are specializing in obtaining used guns for parts salvage.

SEMI-AUTOMATIC SHOTGUNS   The first successful auto-loading shotgun was the Browning. This was marketed in the United States as the Remington Model 11, made under Browning patents. Browning retained the right to sell the gun over the rest of the world, and it was sold there as a Browning. The Remington Model 11, the Browning Automatic, the Savage Automatic, and the Stevens Automatic are all very similar, and anything said about one is true of the others.

The basic mechanism, covered by the wood fore-end, is recoil-operated and has proven to be the most dependable of all auto-loading shotguns. It is specifically known as the long-recoil system, the barrel and the breechblock being locked together all the way back in recoil. When the barrel and the breechblock assembly reaches its rearmost position, the barrel is released from the bolt and snaps forward to its original position. While the barrel is moving forward, the empty shell is held in the breechblock by means of double extractors.

When the barrel reaches its most forward position, the empty shell is thrown out of the gun by means of the ejector attached to the barrel extension. As the barrel returns to position, it trips the mechanism which allows the breechblock to be pushed forward by the recoil spring contained in the butt-stock. This picks up a new shell and feeds it into the barrel. When the breechblock contacts the breech end of the barrel, it is securely locked again into position and again ready to fire. The whole cycle is repeated each time the trigger is pulled, and actually the action is so fast that it is hard for the eye to follow it.

The barrel itself is moved forward by means of a heavy spring around the magazine tube, which extends under the barrel inside the fore-end. There is a ring solidly attached to the bottom of the barrel, which fits around the magazine tube, acting as a guide. Between this solid ring or bracket and the recoil spring there is a friction ring which is adjustable for light and heavy loads. The accompanying diagram shows how these cones are adjusted for different type loads.

The bronze friction piece is split on one side and has a steel spring around the outside, also split to correspond to the split

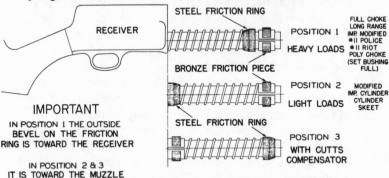

Illustration of proper friction ring adjustments for the long-recoil semi-automatic shotgun. For proper control of recoil and best functioning of the gun, these rings must be properly positioned in relation to the kind of load to be used.

in the friction ring. This spring serves to contract the split bronze ring to a slightly smaller size, so that it has to be slightly "stretched" in order to slip it over the magazine tube. Being under tension of the spring, a friction is created between the bronze piece and the magazine tube.

It is very important to adjust this recoil ring properly for the shell to be used. If it is not properly adjusted, it will either not function or the action will be damaged by excessive recoil. When properly adjusted, the springs and inertia of the recoiling parts will be sufficient to arrest the backward travel of the barrel and the breechblock assembly so that it will stop without slamming into the rear of the receiver. An indication of proper adjustment can be seen by watching ejection. If the friction ring is too loose, the empty shell will be thrown several yards out of the gun and recoil against the shooter's shoulder will be excessive. If the ring is too tight, the mechanism will not travel all the way back and this will cause stoppage. If properly adjusted, the shell will be thrown out a few feet showing that recoil is sufficient to eject the shell but not enough to damage the action.

The other type of auto-loading shotgun is gas-operated. The mechanism of this type of gun is operated by means of a gas piston connected with the bore of the gun by means of a hole or gas port. This type of gun also uses a form of recoil spring which is compressed by the movement of the piston as it is being forced to the rear by the pressure of the gas which enters the gas chamber after the shot charge has passed over the port in the barrel. The operation is quite similar to that of the gas-operated automatic or semi-automatic rifle.

The auto-loading shotgun having only one barrel is subject to the same limitations as the one-barreled pumpgun. Extra barrels and barrel-extension assemblies are available for all auto-loading guns, making it possible to have barrels with different degrees of choke, or any of several adjustable-choke devices can be installed to suit the kind of hunting or shooting contemplated.

CHAPTER **6**

Simple
Shotgun
Repairs

IN REPAIRING many old shotguns, there is one main difficulty encountered—finding replacement parts. New parts are seldom available from the companies that built the guns. Fortunately, there are some companies which are manufacturing parts for old guns, and there are some companies which are making a business of scrapping old guns in order to supply good used parts. You will find parts sources included in the list of suppliers.

Single- and Double-Barrel Shotgun Problems

LOOSE BARREL   Some of the old double-barrel shotguns become very loose—that is, the barrel does not lock tightly into the frame. The fine old shotguns like the A.H. Fox, the L.C. Smith, the Parker and others of this class seldom develop this looseness. If you have one of these good guns that has become loose, you should take it to a good gunsmith and have him make the parts to make it right.

But there are a lot of other shotguns that have become loose, which the amateur can make tight by the methods used by some of the oldtime gunsmiths. Sometimes they would use a light hammer and peen all around the standing breech— where the barrel joins the breech. This would extrude the metal just enough so that the barrel would not close. Then the metal was dressed off with a fine file until the barrel would just close nicely and lock tightly into place. This, of course, did not correct any headspace problem which might have been caused by the loose barrel, but it did tighten things up for a while.

Another way to tighten the barrel was to peen the metal of the hook or barrel lug on which there is a semi-circular cut (a half-hole) which engages the main hinge-pin through the front end of the frame, the pin around which the barrels hinge when the gun is opened or closed. A good way to peen this part is to use the round end of a small ballpeen and tap it with another hammer. This allows the metal around the hinge recess to be drawn out enough to tighten up the barrels to a point where they will not completely close. Do this on both sides of the lug. The lug must be supported on a solid surface. Then the surfaces are dressed off.

Another way in common use employs a center or prick-punch. However, this leaves more unsightly marks than does a small ballpeen hammer. A punch with a round end is another alternative.

Once the metal has been drawn out to a point where the barrel will not completely close, the hinge recess is then dressed out very carefully with a fine round file. This is done by filing, a little at a time, until the gun will just close and lock securely. Sometimes the hook can be bent down slightly by using a copper hammer or a copper punch. The barrel must be placed on a chunk of lead which is soft enough to protect it from becoming bent or disfigured.

In some shotguns, the metal of the locking lug can be drawn out in the same way as was described for the hinge recess, which will make the sliding locking-bolt fit tightly enough to lock the barrel securely in position.

LOOSE FORE-END   Sometimes the fore-end becomes loose. Many of the older double and single-barrel shotguns used a somewhat semi-circular-shaped spring to hold the fore-end securely to the barrel. Sometimes these springs can be removed and straightened a bit to lengthen them and make the fore-end tight when snapped into position. Since these springs are different shapes, they each need a different treatment. Usually they are not hard enough to break, but if they do, they must be replaced. Sometimes a spring may be lengthened slightly by placing it on a flat surface with the spring bridging upward, a hammer then being used to tap and straighten it slightly.

Some shotgun fore-ends are held in place with a coil spring and plunger arrangement. Sometimes it is possible to replace the spring with a little stronger one.

BROKEN FIRING-PIN   One of the most common troubles with single and double-barrel guns is a broken firing-pin. A round firing-pin can be made in the same way that was described for making round firing-pins for rifles in chapter 3. You can secure some firing-pins from the supply companies listed who are furnishing parts for old guns. Some of the gun suppliers have complete firing-pin assortments if you are going to need quite a few. One of the best of these assortments is furnished by Brownell. It consists of a wide variety of firing-pins for single-barrel and double-barrel guns, both old and new models.

Usually the firing-pin is a part which is easy to get out of the gun though some can be rather difficult. The firing-pin in some of these old guns is held in place by a retaining pin or a retaining screw. These small retaining screws can usually be replaced by making new ones from standard screws. Often the

6-32 screw can be cut to the proper length and the original hole rethreaded for the new one. Standard machine-screw taps are available in almost any hardware, department or mail-order store at a rather low price. Machine screws are available in flat-head, fillister-head or round-head varieties from almost any nut and bolt supply house or wholesale hardware. It is well to have a supply of small screws on hand. They come in lengths up to one inch, and it is well to get the long ones so that they can be cut to the proper length for any particular work. For gun work, screws larger than #10 are seldom needed. Common sizes are 3-48, 4-40, 6-32 and 10-32; and the fillister head is the type most commonly used in gun work.

MISSING FRONT SIGHTS   Often front sights are missing and these are easily replaced using any of the commercial brands of front sights. These are furnished in various sizes of beads as well as in various shank sizes, and they can be obtained with matching taps and drills. They are listed in the catalogs of the various supply houses.

Most of the older single- and double-barrel shotguns used flat springs. Spring assortments are available from most of the supply houses. They cost about $3 and various sizes of flat material are supplied. Some of these supply houses have special roughed-out springs which can be fitted to some guns. Send description of the gun and the part needed to Christy, Numrich, Wolff or Martin Retting.

Pumpgun Problems

Pump-action shotguns often need repair, but for these guns this is relatively difficult without having extensive equipment. All auto-loading and repeating shotguns use the tubular-magazine principle. If the tube becomes dented, the dents can be removed in the same way as described for tubular magazines in rifles. (See chapter 3).

In all shotguns of the repeating variety, the extractor spring may become jammed due to dirt or rust. If this occurs, the spring must be removed, the recess cleaned, and the spring repaired if necessary.

Some repeating shotguns utilize wire springs; new ones are easily made out of piano wire which is available from hardware suppliers.

There are many small flat springs used in various pumpguns, some of which can be made out of pieces of clock spring.

A number of gunsmith supply houses carry a special annealed flat spring material, from which it is quite easy to shape some types of flat springs. Then this material can be heat-treated by using the largest tip of the Prest-O-Lite torch or gasoline torch. The heat-treatment depends on the type of steel and usually the supplier will furnish heat-treating directions. A plain carbon spring steel is easily heat-treated by the old flash-off method. The spring is bent and fashioned to the shape desired, and then heated to a cherry red and quenched in oil. One of the best oils for this heat-treating is ordinary cooking oil such as Mazola, Crisco, etc., or raw linseed oil. After the spring has been heated to cherry-red and quenched in oil and has become cool from the action of the oil, it is removed and "flashed off." This means that the oil adhering to the spring is burned off by again applying heat. The spring is heated evenly until the oil begins to burn, and held in various positions until the oil is all burned off. It is then again quenched in oil. This requires a little practice so as to get the proper temper with the various steels. Sometimes thin springs require flashing-off only once, while heavier springs may require it two or three times. When finished, the spring should be soft enough so that it can be filed. If it is so hard that it cannot be filed, the spring will break. As previously mentioned, this requires considerable practice, but excellent springs can be made with a little experience.

EXAMPLES—TYPICAL WINCHESTERS The M97 shotgun is probably the most famous and most durable as well as the strongest of all the pump-action shotguns. Its predecessor was known as the M1893, and was made for black powder only. Between 30,000 and 40,000 of the M1893 were manufactured, and because of its success and popularity, the Model 97 was developed. The 97 is similar to the 93, but with many improvements. It is strong enough to actually withstand high-pressure rifle cartridges. This is not to say that this action is adapted for rifle cartridges, but it has been proven by actual trial that it is strong enough. The M97 is still in great demand by some sportsmen especially because it is one of the most reliable actions ever produced. There were something over a million of the M97 shotguns made between 1897 and 1956. Because of their extreme durability, a very high percentage of these are still in use and will be for some time.

However, there are a few things that happen to this gun now and then, and which require fixing.

1. Failure of action to lock. This can be caused by dirt in the action. Some of these guns have been used for so many years without the action being thoroughly cleaned that an accumulation of dirt has built up in various places, enough to cause the action to fail to lock. One trouble spot is the slide-bar cam lug which sometimes becomes worn enough so that the action will not stay securely locked.

The first thing to do about this is to dissassemble the action and boil all parts in some good cleaning solution such as Oakite or lye. This may clear up the trouble entirely, but if it is necessary to build up this lug, it is necessary to build it up with a welding torch. This is best done only by a competent welder. Usually it is possible to secure an old catalog or parts list showing the shape of the various parts and such diagrams are of help to anyone building up or making new parts.

2. Looseness in frame. The older M97 shotguns were solid-frame, but the highest percentage incorporate the take-

down feature. Sometimes the block becomes loose in the frame or receiver. If so, this can easily be tightened by moving the bolt-adjustment bushing. The latter is simply a sleeve screwed onto the barrel and threaded on the outside with a half or interrupted thread. It is fitted with notches on one side which are engaged by a small lug which, in turn, is held in place by a small screw. The small slide or lug can be loosened so as to disengage from the notches, thus allowing the sleeve to turn freely. Turn the slide one or two notches and lock it in place; then replace barrel and receiver. If it is not tight, move the sleeve another notch or two.

The Model 12 Winchester now and then requires the same tightening treatment, depending on amount of use.

3. Failure to fire. There is a screw in the rear end of the triggerguard which is accessible only when the stock is removed. This screw extends through the triggerguard and contacts the trigger where it acts to prevent the trigger from coming back too far after firing. As the gun becomes worn and dirt accumulates, the gun may fail to fire when the trigger is pulled. This leaves the gun in a *fully-cocked position*, but since it doesn't fire the gun, the first thing the shooter usually does is try to work the action by pulling the forearm back which will cause the gun to *accidentally discharge.* This is because the trigger comes back and strikes the screw before the hammer releases. To remedy this, the stock must be removed and the adjusting screw backed off a turn or two. An alternative correction, for example if the stock has a cemented pad which cannot be removed, is to file off a little bit of the end of the screw which will allow the trigger to come back far enough to release the hammer.

4. Failure to extract. Extraction troubles in this gun are about of the same varieties as for the other guns mentioned. This includes broken extractors, jammed extractor springs and plungers. The broken or weak parts or springs must be replaced.

5. Failure to eject. The ejector in the Model 97 has a small L-shaped spring, which is held in place by a screw in the upper left-hand side of the receiver. The small end of the ejector spring extends through a hole in the receiver and serves to kick the fired shell out of the gun. This spring often breaks, but it can easily be repaired without taking the gun apart.

The carrier is composed of several parts including the hammer, the mainspring, the sear, the sear spring, etc. As the action is opened, the carrier assembly drops out of the bottom of the action. A great amount of dirt can accumulate inside the carrier assembly and may become great enough to prevent the sear from engaging the hammer. The remedy is to remove the carrier assembly, disassemble it, and clean it thoroughly.

6. Failure to feed. Some feeding difficulties are the same as for other pump actions, such as: dents in the magazine tube, which are removed in the same way as suggested for dents in tubular rifles in chapter 3; rusted follower and spring, which is cured by polishing the carrier and replacing the carrier spring; and broken shell-stop spring, which is a flat spring and a new one can easily be made out of spring-steel stock.

7. Failure to stay cocked. The sear spring, which can be seen from the lower side of the gun, fits into a recess in the bottom of the carrier. This, too, is a flat spring which sometimes breaks. A replacement can be made out of regular spring stock but it requires filing to shape, because it is a sort of tapered spring with a thick end, which is drilled and counter-bored for the retaining screw. The spring can be made out of 1/16 in. or ⅛ in. flat spring stock and tempered by the flash-off or burning-off method described earlier in this chapter.

The Model 12 Winchester was probably the most popular pumpgun ever manufactured. It was first produced in 1912 and discontinued in 1965. It developed difficulties of about the same pattern as the other pump-action shotguns.

1. Failure to lock: The breechbolt of the M12 is locked into a recess on the top of the receiver. Sometimes this recess

becomes clogged with dirt, thus preventing the breechblock from completely locking. The remedy for this is a thorough cleaning.

This trouble could also be caused by a damaged or broken slide cam lug. If this lug is burred or upset, it can usually be cleaned up with a file, but if it is broken, it must be replaced. Some parts are available from companies specializing in used or obsolete parts.

2. Loose lug. Sometimes the fore-end, as it is pushed away, will go too far forward. Ordinarily, this forward travel is stopped by a lug which consists of a short piece of metal brazed or soldered around the magazine tube. If this lug comes loose, thus allowing the fore-end to go too far forward, it must be re-silver-soldered or brazed to its original position.

3. Failure to extract. In this model the ejector is a separate piece which fits into the inside of the receiver. There is a small, flat spring attached to the back side of the ejector and this spring sometimes breaks. A replacement spring is easily made.

EXAMPLES—TYPICAL REMINGTONS Among the obsolete pump-action shotguns are the M10 and M29 Remington. Parts are unavailable except for a few of the most common. The Model 10 is a difficult gun to work on. With few exceptions, an amateur should avoid work on these models.

Sometimes ejection and feeding problems are caused by breakage of the flat spring called the ejector spring. New ejector springs are available from Christy and probably from other firms that specialize in parts for obsolete guns. Numrich Arms is always a good source for obsolete parts.

The cartridge carrier also gives a great deal of trouble—another parts replacement problem.

PROBLEMS IN OTHER PUMPGUNS There were large numbers of Stevens shotguns manufactured, and lower-priced models of these guns were marketed under the name "Springfield." For example, the Springfield autoloading shotgun was practically identical to the Savage autoloader and the Remington M11. These same models were made for various mail-order companies. Many of these were sold by Sears under the name "Ranger," and by Montgomery Ward under the name "Western Field." Most of these were based on Browning patents and the pumpgun locking systems were generally similar to the autoloading system in principle except that their mechanisms were hand rather than recoil-operated. Many of the malfunctions of these models follow about the same pattern as those of the autoloaders and gas-operated shotguns, such as broken extractors, broken firing-pins, etc.

Another popular pumpgun is the Ithaca M37 and its predecessor, the Remington M17. Under normal conditions, both of these models are reliable. Mechanically simple, they are different from most other pump-action guns in that they load and eject through the bottom. Several malfunctions are easily repaired.

1. Breechblock fails to lock. This may be due to burrs on the locking surfaces, which can easily be removed; or dirt may have built up in the locking recess in the top of the receiver or in the extractor holes in the breech-end of the barrel.

2. Double-Feeding. May be caused by worn right-hand cartridge stop. This calls for the installation of a new part.

3. Extraction failure. Can be caused by a broken extractor or a broken extractor spring.

Semi-Automatic Shotgun Maintenance

LONG-RECOIL SEMI-AUTOMATICS   The Model 11 Remington with its companion gun known as the "Sportsman" is one of the most common semi-automatic shotgun designs. There are many other makes which use essentially the same design, and the experiences with the Model 11 are more or less common to other similar guns such as the Savage Automatic, the Browning Automatic and the Stevens Automatic, all made under the Browning patent. Some troubles common to the automatic shotguns are caused by improper adjustment of the friction ring. This adjustment is illustrated in the previous chapter under Semi-Automatic Shotguns. This reference should be carefully studied by anyone owning one of these automatics.

There are numerous things which cause automatic shotguns of this type not to operate well.

1. Failure of the action to close. If the action fails to close, it may be caused by the cartridge stop not releasing the new shell. This requires replacement of the cartridge stop.

The extractor hook may have a sharp corner which catches the rim of the shell as it is being fed up. Such a sharp corner can be removed with a small file.

If the shell catches the lower edge of the chamber, thus preventing the shell from feeding into the barrel, the lower edge of the chamber can be chamfered (beveled) slightly to relieve the sharp corner.

Sometimes the barrel will get out of alignment, which will cause the barrel extension to get into the path of the breechblock, so that the ejector causes the breechblock to jam. This is caused by the magazine tube being out of alignment, and can be corrected by straightening the magazine tube.

2. Sticking of barrel in action. Sometimes the barrel will stick back in the action. This may be caused by the magazine tube being dry or rough, thus increasing friction between the magazine tube and the friction piece. This can be remedied by polishing and oiling the magazine tube. Sometimes the friction ring will become so dry that the magazine will not fully open, or will not open far enough to lock the breechblock back. Oil the friction piece.

Sometimes the barrel is out of alignment because of a bent magazine tube. To remedy, bend the magazine tube near the receiver in the opposite direction to the way the barrel seems to point when one sights the gun.

The cycle of these guns is quite complex. When the gun fires, the barrel-extension and the breechblock remain locked together and travel all the way back to the end of the receiver at which point the breechblock and the breechblock assembly is locked in the rearmost position. At this point the recoil spring around the magazine tube takes over and pulls the barrel and the barrel-extension to the most forward position. But just as they reach this point, the breechblock is tripped and moves forward from the action of the recoil spring and stock to again load the barrel.

3. Ejection failure. Obviously, if there is something to prevent the breechblock from coming back far enough to lock, the empty shell will not be ejected and the gun will have to be loaded manually to again operate.

Sometimes the various levers and notches may cause the breechblock not to lock. This can be checked by placing the muzzle of the gun on a wood floor and pushing down on the stock and receiver until the barrel and breechblock assembly are in their rearmost position. Then pressure can be eased up so that the barrel will move forward so that one can see whether the breechblock is locked back or not. If the gun fails to eject, the ejector may be broken or loosened from the barrel and extension. This require replacement of the ejector.

4. Failure to extract. If the gun fails to extract, the extractor may be broken and must be replaced. Or, the extractor spring may be caught or stuck back in its recess, allowing the extractor to slip off the shell. To remedy this, the extractor spring hole should be cleaned out and the spring, with a drop of oil on it, should be replaced. The oil is to prevent rust.

The extractor claw may become dull and slip off the fired shell. If this happens, the extractor should be replaced. A weak or jammed extractor can also cause this trouble.

5. Failure to feed. If the shell fails to feed into the barrel, the cartridge-stop arm may be bent out of adjustment. The remedy for this is to bend the arm toward its center.

The carrier latch may have been bent too near the center of the arm at the front end. To remedy this, bend the front end of the carrier farther away from the center of the arm.

Another cause of failure to feed is that sometimes the front end of the carrier is adjusted too high and thus intercepts the shell coming out of the magazine. To correct, bend the front end of the carrier downward.

Dents or dirt in the magazine tube may prevent the shells from coming back into the receiver. To remedy this, the tube should be thoroughly cleaned and any noticeable dents raised.

The carrier dog may not be adjusted properly to hold the carrier up against the bottom of the shell, allowing the shell to strike against the edge of the chamber. The remedy for this is to adjust the carrier dog so that it raises the carrier higher.

6. Misfires. If the gun misfires, it may be due to a broken firing-pin. Some of these guns have a firing-pin that is very hard to make because it has a large square end. The best answer is a new part. If the pin is round, the amateur may be able to file this out as described for the other round pins. (See chapter 3.)

A broken mainspring may cause misfires. This requires replacement of the mainspring.

7. Repeats firing automatically. If the gun empties itself with one pull of the trigger, the trigger notches may be out of adjustment with the hammer. This requires readjustment of the trigger to the hammer. If the rear notch of the trigger or the notch of the hammer are worn, these notches may be sharpened but often a new hammer or a new trigger is required.

Another cause of this trouble is a safety sear which may have become worn or broken. This requires a new part.

8. Timing out. Another common ailment of this kind of automatic shotgun is a battered fore-end. The fore-end not only works as a fore-end, but it also acts as a spacer to properly relate the barrel and barrel-extension to the other parts as the

gun functions. If the fore-end wood has become so oil-soaked or battered that the barrel-extension protrudes noticeably beyond the end of the receiver, the fore-end should be replaced. For old models, these may be difficult to find. One of the best suppliers for these parts is Sile Distributors (See list of suppliers).

THE GAS-OPERATED SHOTGUNS   All automatic arms are at times tempermental under conditions that would have no effect whatsoever on the performance of a manually-operated repeater. They are often sensitive to the variations in thickness of various makes of shells, to differences in condition of old or new shells, to heavy oils or no oil at all, to blistering heat and freezing cold, etc. So with these guns regular cleaning and oiling of the mechanisms is necessary if they are to operate properly. The Remington factory recommends the use of an evaporating solvent, used with care, as "action mechanisms remain clean much longer after shooting if the lubricant is used sparingly."*

Special care must be taken that oil is removed from the action parts when the weather is below freezing. If some lubricant then is still desired, use dry graphite. But care must also be taken to prevent rusting from condensation and wetness on action parts, and the bore and chamber as well, when guns are taken from cold weather into warm room temperatures.

TYPICAL REPAIRS   The most common gas-operated shotguns are the M1100 Remington and the M50 Winchester. The M50 has what might be described as a floating-chamber, while the Remington M1100 has a gas cylinder and a piston.

The mechanism of these guns often becomes fouled with powder residue and dried oil, thus preventing complete operation of the action. There is a service manual for the M50 Winchester available from the Winchester factory which gives complete instructions and diagrams for disassembly and reas-

*Remington Instruction Folder—M1100

sembly of this action.

There are some common failures, but most are closely related to the cleaning and oiling.

1. Failure of bolt to close. This can be caused by a simple lack of oil or an accumulation of dirt.

2. Failure to eject. Remove guard; oil inertia-rod, slide cuts in the receiver, and cam-slots in the bolt. Use oil moderately. Broken springs, firing-pins etc, such as are common to all repeating shotguns must be replaced.

The M1100 Remington is operated by means of a piston rather than by a floating-chamber, and its gas cylinder is permanently attached to the barrel. There is a gas port leading into the barrel near the front end of the fore-end. When the gun is fired the gas passes through the port into the gas cylinder with sufficient force to drive the piston to the rear, thus operating the action in almost exactly the same manner as does the manually-operated fore-end on a pump gun.

Part of the Remington instructions for disassembly of this gun for cleaning is as follows:

Use evaporating solvent.

Trigger plate assembly—Push safety ON SAFE. Close action. Tap out front and rear trigger-plate pins. Remove trigger-plate assembly from receiver. Inspect and brush clean whenever necessary. Clean as a unit. Do not allow cocked hammer to snap forward with trigger-plate assembly, breech bolt or barrel removed from receiver of gun.

Breech bolt assembly-Gas mechanism. Push safety ON SAFE. Close action. Unscrew magazine cap. Remove fore-end and barrel. Pull out operating handle. Remove barrel seal, piston and piston seal from magazine tube. Separate barrel seal slightly to ease removal. Reach into carrier opening from beneath receiver and depress feed-latch in receiver. Pull action-bar sleeve, action-bar assembly and attached breechbolt from receiver and magazine tube. Lift breech bolt (and attached locking block) from rear of bar.

Feed latch must be pressed again to allow re-entry of action-bar assembly and breech bolt to receiver. Make certain piston-seal, piston and barrel-seal are in correct assembly position when replacing.

When cleaning, brush or scrape to remove shooting residue, if necessary. Wipe all parts clean, including gas cylinder attached to barrel and magazine tube. After cleaning gas mechanism parts, wipe clean and dry. Use as little oil as possible.

CHAPTER 7

Handguns and Their Intricacies

MODERN HANDGUNS can be roughly divided into three classes: Single-Shots, Automatics and Revolvers.

Single-Shot Pistols

There are countless designs of single-shot pistols. The company making the largest number of models is probably the J. Stevens Arms Company. This company manufactured handguns of all types and descriptions, most being built on the tip-up type of action. Some of these pistols were made with large barrels and skeleton stocks, sometimes described as "bicycle rifles" or "pocket rifles." Some were made for the .410 shotshell. The latter are illegal since the enactment of the Federal Firearms Act. The standard Stevens tip-up model, having the appearance of the automatic pistol, had the fault of having the front sight on the barrel and the rear sight on the receiver. Consequently, when the barrel became loose, it became inaccurate. The last tip-up models manufactured, known as the Stevens Off-Hand model, have both sights mounted on the barrel and they were unaffected by any looseness of the locking system.

Later, the Harrington and Richardson Company made a model known as the U.S.R.A. model. This gun was quite popular during the Thirties and possibly could be called the most accurate handgun ever produced in the United States. It was manufactured for only a short period of time and good specimens are avidly sought at present.

Lately, new single-shot pistols are being introduced. "The Contender," manufactured by the Thompson Center Arms Company, appears to be a very interesting gun, since it can be purchased with a set of interchangeable barrels made for different cartridges—the .22 Long Rifle, the .22 WMR, the .22 Jet, the .22 Hornet, the .38 Special, the .256 Win., the .357 Magnum, the .45 Colt, the .45 Colt/.410, the .45 ACP, and the .17 Bumblebee. Barrels for additional calibers quite possibly are on the way. Among the other single-shot pistols is the XP100 Remington bolt-action pistol (unusual) chambered for the .221 Fireball. Single-shot pistols are inherently more accurate than an automatic or revolver because they have no cylinder to line up with the barrel as is the case with a revolver, or no sights in two different parts—one of which moves—as in the case of the average .22 automatic pistol where the sights are often even mounted on a loose-fitting slide covering a relatively loose barrel. They also have the advantage of accepting bottleneck cartridges such as the .256 Winchester, which will not work well in an ordinary revolver because the bottleneck cartridge tends to freeze the cylinder, preventing it from turning to the next round.

Semi-Automatic Pistols

The automatic pistol is actually a semi-automatic requiring a separate pull of the trigger for each shot, just as in the semi-automatic rifle. The magazine of most automatics is the clip type, holding from five to twelve shots, and most automatics have a provision for containing such a magazine in the grip.

Automatic pistols made for rimfire cartridges and the less powerful center-fire cartridges, use the simple blowback system. There is no locking system except the simple inertia or weight of the slide plus the recoil spring. The slide sometimes extends over the entire barrel, sometimes only over the receiver. For example, all of the better .22 automatic pistols, with the exception of the small pocket guns, are made with a stationary barrel screwed into the receiver in the same fashion as a rifle barrel, with the slide and operating mechanism extending to the rear. Examples of this type of gun are the Ruger .22 Automatic Pistol, the Smith & Wesson .22 Automatic, the High Standard, the Colt, the Star, and many others. These are very accurate, trouble-free pistols, handling the popular .22 L.R. cartridges.

Examples of pistols having a slide extending the entire length of the gun with the barrel inside are the .45 M1911A1 (U.S.) automatic pistol, the Smith & Wesson Model 39 and numerous Spanish and European pistols of the same type. Most of these pistols, being chambered for the more powerful center-fire pistol cartridges, have some form of delayed blowback action system, which means that it is a locked-breech system, activated by the barrel and slide assembly moving back a short distance while they are locked together. When the assembly reaches the end of this preliminary action (which is only a fraction of an inch, but which gives the bullet time to clear the muzzle) the barrel and slide unlock from each other, allowing the slide to continue to the rear through its full cycle. As the slide returns into the battery position, it picks up a fresh cartridge from the clip magazine, feeds it into the barrel, locks the mechanism and the pistol is ready to fire again.

An example of a high-powered automatic pistol having a stationary barrel is the Luger. It is a delayed blowback and is of the toggle-joint type, which permits the breechblock mechanism to move up as well as back. It is a very strong action and will accept relatively powerful, bottleneck, center-fire cartridges.

It is quite difficult to get a good trigger pull on most automatic pistols as is on the other hand possible with either the single-shot or the single-action revolver.

Revolvers

Capable of holding several cartridges in its cylinder, usually six but sometimes eight or nine, a revolver is a repeating handgun in which the cylinder is rotated to ready successive shots for firing. Revolvers are generally referred to as being of two styles—single-action and double-action.

The single-action requires that the hammer be pulled back by the thumb to full cock before it can be fired, while the double-action revolver can be both cocked and discharged by one pull of the trigger. By cocking the hammer by hand, the double-action can be, and usually is, used as a single-action. But the double-action can generally be fired more rapidly than the single-action by simply pulling the trigger, which cocks the hammer, turns the cylinder and fires the gun as the result of the one long pull of the trigger. For the average individual, double-action firing is difficult to control and very little accuracy can be realized this way in spite of Western movies and television shows in which the "good guy" can light a match at fifty paces, while the "bad guy" will miss a barn door at the same distance. Law enforcement agents are trained to use a double-action revolver skilfully, but there is not much need for a sportsman to develop such skill.

Normally a better trigger pull can be attained on a single-shot action, since it is a simpler mechanism consisting of a trigger and sear which engages directly into the hammer notch, thus elminating the double-action. The single-action is also more reliable because its parts are more rugged and more positive in their action.

It is obvious that for any degree of accuracy, the revolver's cylinder and barrel must be held to exact alignment. If they are not, the bullet will be shaved slightly on one side and will wobble. New guns of cheap construction may not line up correctly, and nothing can be done about these. But good guns may develop poor alignment as a result of long wear. These can sometimes be corrected by the installation of a new cylinder hand, the part that pushes the cylinder around into place for each shot. Sometimes it is also necessary to replace the ratchet at the end of the cylinder.

Revolvers and single-shot pistols are much safer weapons to use than the automatic pistol. The single-shot must be reloaded by hand for each shot and it usually has a visible hammer which tells at a glance if it is ready to fire. The same is true of a revolver. On the other hand, many automatic pistols are of the hammerless variety; such a gun does not show to the person picking up the gun whether or not it is loaded, and usually its safety mechanism is not too glaringly visible. This makes it very possible for an inexperienced person or a child to pick it up and fire it, and then, with only a touch of the finger, it is ready to fire again. The better automatic pistols lock open after the last cartridge is fired, and some automatic pistols, such as the .45 Colt Automatic Pistol, have outside hammers.

There is currently a trend to produce more and more powerful pistol cartridges with big heavy revolvers being made to accept them. Many articles are written about how efficient these big handguns are for big-game hunting. This idea should be dispelled right here, because for too many readers the reaction might be for one to think he can just go to a store, procure a big handgun and kill an elephant the first shot. In reality most shooters find it hard to defend themselves with a .45 Automatic. Such a pistol is very difficult to shoot with accuracy because of its recoil and muzzle-blast. Stories describing pistol kills on big game at distances up to five or six hundred yards are feats maybe possible only for the real expert, but even these experts shoot their pistols with two hands, or over a log to help steady the gun, or by some means other than from a standing position. If two hands are to be needed, for shooting purposes, it is better to get a rifle and confine handgun shooting to its more practical aspects. Some states have enacted laws against the use of handguns in hunting big game in order to prevent wounding too many game animals. And this is as it should be.

The most practical pistols are probably the ones chambered for the .22 Long Rifle. It is sufficiently powerful for anything that should be hunted with a handgun. It is relatively easy to shoot and is relatively economical. It is surprisingly powerful in comparison with some larger cartridges. It is one of the best game-stoppers when you consider that it is easier to make a *good* hit with it than with heavier pieces of hand artillery.

CHAPTER 8

Simple Repairs— Colt and S&W Types

HIGH-GRADE revolvers can often be repaired without the use of expensive tools.

Single-Action

A single-action Colt has an extremely simple mechanism, but it has certain weaknesses which may require parts repair or new parts.

1. Failure to lock cylinder. The part which locks the cylinder in alignment is activated by one prong of a flat spring; the other prong works the trigger. This lock is called the cylinder bolt and when it fails to lock the cylinder, it is almost always an indication of a broken spring. To repair this, first remove the backstrap which will expose the main or hammer spring, which can then be easily removed. Then remove the three screws holding the triggerguard to the bottom of the frame. This will allow the triggerguard (which includes the lower

tang or grip, the triggerguard bow and a sort of floorplate) to come free, uncovering the bottom of the action and exposing the two-prong cylinder and bolt spring, which is held in place by one screw. Remove the screw and replace the spring with a new one, making sure that each prong is in proper position, one bearing on the cylinder bolt and the other on the trigger. Reassemble the gun and the job is finished.

2. Handspring Breakage. The single-action Colt is also prone to handspring breakage. This can always be diagnosed by holding the gun with the muzzle straight down and cocking the hammer, at the same time, watching the cylinder turn; then repeat the operation with the muzzle of the gun straight up. If the handspring is broken, the cylinder will not turn since the broken handspring is not holding the hand against the ratchet. To install a new spring, the hammer must be removed. To do this the triggerguard and mainspring must be removed as described above. Then remove the two-pronged trigger and bolt spring, and the bolt and trigger which are held in place by two screws through the frame. Then the hammer, including the hand and the handspring can be pushed down through the frame. This spring is held in place by means of a slot in the hand, and the old spring can be pushed out by a punch and the new spring driven into position. Then reassemble to the hammer and push the assembly back into the frame.

3. End-play in the cylinder. Often the cylinder of the Single-Action Colt will develop end-play due to wear on the end of the base-pin bushing. This is a cylindrical tube which fits through the center of the cylinder, acting as a bearing on which the cylinder turns on the base pin. The main pin holding the cylinder in place is called the base pin. The base-pin bushing can usually be pushed out of the cylinder by means of a punch which is larger than the hole in the bushing, but smaller than the hole in the cylinder. A new base-pin bushing can be obtained from the factory or a gunsmith supplier. If this bushing is too long to fit into the frame, it is necessary

to trim it to fit by filing the front end of the bushing to a point where it will slip into the frame, but being very careful not to file off enough to cause end-play.

Sometimes the old base-pin bushing may be the proper length, but the hole may have become worn, thus allowing the cylinder to wobble. This requires the replacement of the base-pin bushing and sometimes the base pin.

4. Broken firing-pin. The firing-pin of the old Single-Action Colt is of the fixed type held in the hammer by means of a retaining pin through the hammer. This pin fits so closely that sometimes it is hard to see. Drive out this pin with the proper-size punch. Then, through the hole in the back side of the hammer, push out the old firing-pin. The new firing-pin can then be pushed into the hammer and the retaining pin driven back in.

5. Broken recoil plate. Sometimes the recoil plate breaks loose. This is a small circular part which fits around the firing-pin and is crimped into place. This can be tightened, but it is best done by a competent gunsmith who has the proper tools.

Christy furnishes a patented firing-pin which comes as an assembly and requires the removal of the original fixed firing-pin. It extends through the frame in such a manner that the hammer can strike the new pin. This must be installed by a competent gunsmith.

Double-Action Revolvers

The higher-grade, double-action revolvers are usually solid-frame with a swing-out cylinder. The best makes are Colt and Smith & Wesson. The two guns appear quite similar from the outside, but they are quite different mechanisms. The Smith & Wesson is a left-hand wheeler, that is the cylinder turns to the left. The Colt is a right-hand wheeler, that is the cylinder turns to the right or clockwise.

These good revolvers have perfectly-fitting sideplates

which can be removed to expose the entire mechanism. In the
Smith & Wesson, these side plates are held in place by three

The mechanism of a typical Colt double-action revolver.

The mechanism of a typical Smith and Wesson double-action revolver.

screws, with the front screw holding the crane (the frame
holding the cylinder). It is necessary to *put this particular
screw back in this hole*, since it has an extension to fit into the

cut in the crane, which lines up the front sideplate hole. This prevents the crane from moving forward, while at the same time permitting it to swing freely.

Be careful when removing the sideplate, as it may easily be marred or bent out of shape if struck with a hammer or pried upon. Strike the grip frame sharply with a wooden block on the same side as the sideplate. This will usually cause the sideplate to move upward and kick out of its recess. To replace the sideplate of the Smith & Wesson during reassembly, work it forward from the rear of the handspring, for if the sideplate is forward of the handspring, the latter will be ruined when the hammer is cocked.

The Colt revolver is dissassembled by removing parts in the following order: crane-lock screw and crane lock; crane with cylinder; stock screw and stocks, side-plate screws and side plate, hand and handspring, mainspring, hammer, rebound lever and rebound-lever spring, cylinder bolt and spring, trigger, locking lever screw and locking lever, latch pin and latchpin spring. When removing parts they should be carefully put aside so that they can be replaced properly.

A common ailment of the various-model Colts is timing, and the smaller models give more trouble than the larger ones. When a Colt revolver is "out of time," it means that the cylinder does not lock in place when the hammer is cocked in single-action fashion.

To check a double-action for a timing problem, cock the gun very slowly, single-action, until the trigger engages the hammer, holding it back in full-cock position. Then grasp the cylinder and try to turn it back counterclockwise. If the bolt is locked to the cylinder, it will be impossible to move the cylinder backward, indicating that it is perfectly timed. If the cylinder is not locked, it indicates that the cylinder is out of time, or approaching that condition. A further test can be made by cocking the gun a little more vigorously and if the cylinder then locks, it indicates that the gun is not badly out of time and will still operate satisfactorily. Since the hand is attached directly to the trigger, it operates simultaneously with the trigger and usually a Colt double-action revolver, on which the cylinder is not locked when the trigger is pulled, will turn around a little further and fall into locked position before the hammer falls all the way down.

A revolver's being out of time may be due to any one of several things, such as the ratchet being worn, the hand being worn or loose, the hole in the hammer being worn or oversize, the cylinder bolt being worn or loose, etc. As the condition becomes worse, the timing will get so far off that the cylinder never does lock. Then a complete overhaul is necessary.

Sometimes the crane or yoke may be sprung out of line. This is especially true of the Colt revolver in which the cylinder has become loose due to a worn cylinder pin or wear in other parts. But sometimes it is caused by someone trying to tighten the cylinder by deliberately bending the frame. Some so-called gunsmiths stick a screwdriver between the frame and crane, put the gun in a vise and put enough pressure against the cylinder to actually bend the crane inward. This will tighten the cylinder all right, but it will also throw the cylinder out of alignment with the barrel. If the crane has been bent, it is necessary to straighten it or repair it; and then re-time the mechanism.

The Colt hand or pawl differs from the Smith & Wesson in that it has two points, thus it is usually described as a double-hand. As the hammer is cocked, the uppermost part of the hand engages one segment of the ratchet, and as the hammer moves back, this point moves the cylinder part way around, at which time the lower point of the hand comes in contact with the next segment of the ratchet, thus creating the more powerful thrust or a stronger push against the ratchet than can be exercised by the single hand of the Smith and Wesson type. This created a very dependable or positive action, but this design has other failings which more or less offset this admirable feature, as for example, the pins becoming worn or loose so that the gun becomes out of time.

The only repairs that can be made in the home workshop are the replacement of parts, and some of the new parts have to be hand-fitted, which can usually be accomplished by the judicious use of files and hones. It takes considerable experience to fit parts to the Colt action. The cylinder is held in place by the latchpin, and this is the only thing which anchors the cylinder in place while the gun is being operated. The latchpin extends through the frame and is operated by a thumbpiece on the outside of the frame, which when pulled back, pulls the latchpin out of the recess in the center of the ratchet. This recess often becomes worn to such an extent that the cylinder becomes quite loose.

To repair this, a new latchpin can be fitted and sometimes a new ratchet and extractor may have to be installed. The ratchet is screwed onto the ejector rod. To remove it, push the ejector rod back far enough so that it frees the ratchet from the cylinder. Then use a small adjustable wrench to unscrew the ratchet. A new ratchet is then screwed onto the ejector rod, to a position which will allow the ratchet to fit back in the cylinder perfectly.

A worn pin, such as a hammer pin, cylinder-bolt pin or trigger pin, which is pressed into the frame, can be replaced with an oversize pin, but these have to be made and installed by a competent gunsmith who has the necessary equipment. These special pins must be precisely made so that they hold the various parts in place without excessive play or wobble.

Close examination or observation of how each part functions often suggests necessary repairs. The action can be operated slowly while cocking the hammer with one thumb, while at the same time holding the hand down with the other.

One of the things which causes difficulties with the Colt double-action is that so many parts serve two or more functions. The mainspring is of the V-type, with the upper prong operating the hammer and the lower prong operating the rebound lever. The rebound lever is a large bar pinned into the frame toward the lower end of the grip (frame) and extending up to engage into a notch on the inside of the hand, this lever being activated by the lower half of the mainspring, which acts to return the trigger into position, but which, after it has been pulled and loaded, acts as the hammer spring. On the side of the rebound lever is a small projection which engages the end of the cylinder bolt, which trips the bolt out of the recess in the cylinder at the proper time to permit the cylinder to turn freely and as the cycle progresses, the cylinder bolt is released and allowed to drop back against the cylinder and engage in the recess to hold the cylinder in place.

All this requires very accurate timing. It is a rather complicated cycle and as Roy Dunlap says, "It is closely akin to a Rube Goldberg creation." Other than minor adjustments, replacing worn parts, cleaning and oiling, work on the Colt double-action should be left to the expert.

There is one early double-action Colt which is a left-hand wheeler. This double-action model appears to be fairly similar to the more modern ones, but it has been obsolete for many years, and it is very difficult to get parts. This Colt cylinder locks only at the rear by means of a latchpin; the cylinder swings out to the left. The pressure of the hand against the ratchet turns the cylinder to the right, which has a tendency to push the crane and cylinder assembly a little further into the frame. However, with the left-hand wheelers, the tendency is to push the cylinder and the crane away from the frame, thus introducing other complications. These left-hand wheelers are very difficult to repair, and usually the cost of the repair is far beyond the value of the gun. When trading for or buying a Colt revolver, it should always be ascertained whether it is a left-hand or a right-hand wheeler.

When the double-action Colt of the right-hand wheeling style is in good condition and is kept well-oiled, it is an extremely reliable mechanism in spite of its complicated cycle, and it will give a lifetime of service without major trouble. It is when these guns are misused that the repair fun begins.

About Older Colts

Among the older, better models of the Colt revolver manufactured during the last fifty years, are the Army Special, which became the Official Police, and which is still being manufactured, and the Officer's Model, which is essentially the same gun but fitted with target sights. This gun is also still being made.

The Officer's Model has been one of the all-time-great target handguns. Over the years, it has been made in .22 and .38 Special cartridges, and lately the .22 Rimfire Magnum cartridge has been added. The same is true of the Official Police. The main difference between the two guns is the difference in sights, the Official Police having fixed sights, which are more rigid for field use.

The Police Positive and the Police Positive Special were two common models. The latter is still being manufactured in the .32 and .38 calibers. This is a small or light-frame model while the Official Police can be described as a medium-weight-frame model. The old Police Positive which is now extinct, was also made in .22 caliber on a very light frame. A variation of this model is the Detective Special and the Banker's Special which are better described as "belly guns," having very short 2 in. barrels. The mechanisms of these various old-model, double-action Colt revolvers were practically the same except for the size of the parts.

A large-frame, older model Colt revolver was one known as the New Service, and a variation of this model, made for the .45 automatic military cartridge was the 1917 Army Model. The commercial model was always known as the New Service and was chambered for large cartridges like the .45

Colt. The fancy model with target sights added was known as the New Service Target Model.

Thousands of the 1917 Model were sold to the public as surplus and are chambered for the .45 automatic pistol cartridge in conjunction with semicircular clips. It is very difficult to convert one of these cylinders to accept the .45 Colt cartridge. The only way the conversion can be made, practically, is to replace the cylinder with one made for the Colt. Replacement of the cylinder requires a thorough knowledge of the revolver and is beyond the ability of the average amateur and should be done by a competent gunsmith.

Smith and Wesson Principles and Parts

The Smith and Wesson mechanism and cycle of operation is simpler. Each part has only one function to perform. The mainspring is simply a flat spring which operates the hammer directly. There is a rebound spring having a function only to return the trigger and it could very well be called a trigger spring. There is a special small spring which operates the hand.

None of these parts have a tendency to develop wear to a degree which would impair operation of the action. The cylinder is anchored at both ends by a center pin which fits into a recess in the frame. On the bottom of the barrel there is a lug containing a pin and spring. This pin engages the end of the ejector rod, creating a bearing at both ends, thus holding the cylinder in perfect alignment at all times, and these parts are not subject to excessive wear. A Smith & Wesson double-action revolver, when carefully used and cared for, seldom gets out of line or wears enough to destroy its efficiency.

There is, however, a common stoppage which occurs in Smith & Wesson double-action revolvers. The cylinder freezes. This is caused by the ejector rod becoming loose and unscrewing to a point where it binds or freezes against the lug on the

bottom of the barrel. Many unethical gunsmiths have capital-
ized on this one condition. The owner brings the gun to the
gunsmith who looks it over and states that it will have to be
left and he will find the trouble. As soon as the customer
leaves, he will screw in the ejector rod with a pair of pliers
(with a cleaning patch or a cardboard between the jaws of the
pliers to prevent marring the part). Just a partial turn will free
the cylinder and allow it to be unlocked. Then the ejector rod
can be screwed back into place. When the customer returns,
he is charged $5 for some fictitious repair.

There are numerous Smith & Wesson double-action models, but the basic mechanism has never been changed. The
older models come in assorted sizes beginning with the Ladys-
mith, a very small miniature model (which is now very scarce
and worth a great deal) and extending up through the large
1917 Model, which corresponds to the Colt 1917, being also
chambered for the .45 automatic pistol cartridge, and using
the same semicircular clips.

The only basic deviation from this model is the hammerless model. The earliest hammerless was known as the Pocket
Revolver. It was an extremely reliable gun, easily carried in
the pocket because there were no projecting parts, and it was
operated by the double-action method. With a little practice,
these models were capable of very good shooting. Like the
larger, hammer models, very few repairs ever became necessary.

But like all guns, these various models were prone to certain troubles like broken mainsprings and broken firing-pins,
but problems which are easily repaired.

Sometimes misfires occur due to lack of tension on the
mainspring. Most Smith & Wessons are equipped with a *strain
screw* which can be turned in to increase the tension of the
flat mainspring and impart enough force to the falling hammer
to explode the cartridge primers.

The action of the Smith & Wesson can be "balanced" by

carefully adjusting the tension of the mainspring and lightening the rebound or trigger spring. The action of the rebound spring can be lightened by the removal of one or more coils, but it must be done carefully, a little at a time, until it is just the right length to return the trigger to its foremost position. By being very careful in this balancing operation, the trigger pull can be lightened a great deal without touching the sear notch on the trigger and hammer. The reason that this lightens the pull without endangering the safety of the gun is because the rebound or trigger spring does not have to be compressed to any great degree when the trigger is pulled, most of the energy being applied to disengaging the trigger or sear from the hammer. The mainspring is lightened as much as possible and still gives reliable ignition. By carefully making these adjustments, the single-action pull and the double-action pull can be greatly improved.

The firing-pins of the Smith & Wesson come in two styles. The same models, such as the K22, have a separate firing-pin held in place by means of a bushing and a pin, while the other may have a firing pin in the hammer held in place by a pin only. The latter type can be repaired by driving out the firing-pin and replacing it. The other type of firing-pin often breaks. It is easily removed by driving out the retaining pin which passes through the frame and holds the firing-pin bushing in place. When this pin is removed, the firing-pin and bushing can be pushed out of the frame by inserting a small punch through the firing-pin hole in the frame. Usually the old firing-pin will come out by itself without using the punch. The new pin can then be installed and the gun reassembled, being sure that the firing-pin spring is first placed over the firing-pin tip. If this spring is left out, the firing-pin will not be retracted and will stick in the primer, in turn preventing the cylinder from turning.

CHAPTER 9

Repairing
Other
Handguns

THERE ARE thousands and thousands of cheap nickel-plated revolvers, sometimes called Saturday Night Specials, floating around. They are more or less worthless, but they can often be repaired and used as trading stock. Most of these are the break-open type or the even cheaper, solid-frame type.

Cures for Common Faults

1. Cylinder fails to lock. Among the cheap revolvers many have no positive cylinder lock and they can therefore be described as "free-wheelers," but some have a lock which becomes sloppy from wear. A common cause of this trouble is a worn or broken lever spring, called the hand or pawl, which engages the ratchet to turn the cylinder. These are often small flat springs which can be made out of a piece of flat metal such as is found in a spring collection. Some have a wire spring which can easily be made out of a suitable size piano wire which is available from all supply houses.

2. Broken trigger spring. Another common ailment of these revolvers is the trigger spring. These are V-shaped springs which fit in the triggerguard and return the trigger to its foremost position after the trigger is pulled. Since these springs vary greatly in size, shape and thickness, it is necessary to use the old broken spring as a pattern to make a new one. A spring can generally be found in one of the spring assortments which will require only a small amount of work with a file to make it fit or a roughed-out blank can be secured from W.C. Wolff Co. (See list of suppliers.)

The triggerguard is usually held in place by means of two pins or a pin and a screw. In practically all models, the sear pin which holds the triggerguard, also holds the sear in place. When removing the triggerguard, care must be taken to save the sear and the sear pin. It is often found that the sear spring, which is either a small V-shaped spring or a small coil spring, is also broken. Regardless of the type of spring found in the sear, it has to be compressed when the gun is reassembled. The way to do this is to shape a small wooden pin from a matchstick and with it, pin the sear and spring in the recess in the triggerguard. The new trigger spring is then placed in its proper position and the guard pressed into place. This will keep the trigger spring from moving out of position. While holding the triggerguard in place, the rear pin may be inserted in the frame and driven into place. Then the front pin (if there is one) is driven into place. This completes the assembly of the trigger.

3. Misfires. When a revolver misfires, the cause is sometimes a weak mainspring. This is usually a flat spring, the upper end of which fits into the hammer and the lower end fitting into a notch on the lower end of the grip frame. In a collection of mainsprings one can usually be found that will fit with a small amount of alteration, using the old one as a pattern. A roughed-out blank can possibly be secured from Wolff.

If the mainspring is in good condition, misfires are usually caused by a faulty firing-pin. In some revolvers, the firing-pin is attached to the hammer and is made as one-piece with it. These are difficult to repair, but it is possible to split the hammer with a hacksaw and insert a thin piece of steel which can be silver-soldered in place. The lower portion of the hammer can be held in a vise, which will usually draw off the heat to keep the sear notches from becoming softened. But if necessary, the lower part of the hammer can be wrapped in a wet rag, leaving enough of the top exposed to solder. The inserted part should be left larger than necessary and after it has been installed, the hammer is filed to size and shape.

Sometimes the firing-pin, which is one-piece and integral with the hammer, is round and has been broken off. The hammer can then be drilled and a round pin installed and silver-soldered in place. A round pin of this kind can be roughly filed out by chucking it in the electric drill as described in chapter 3, "Making Round Firing-Pins."

Some revolvers have separate firing-pins held in place by bushings, the bushing being held in the frame by means of a cross-pin. These are easily replaced by removing the bushing, with which the firing-pin and the firing-pin spring will come out. There are many types of firing-pins, so that it is necessary to use the old pin as a pattern from which to make the new one. If the tip of the pin is broken off, the new one should be made a little too large and after it has been filed to shape so that it will fit into the bushing freely, the firing-pin tip can be cut to length.

If the pin is for a center-fire revolver, the tip end must be made round or semicircular in shape, while the pin for a rimfire revolver is sometimes wedge-shaped and must be filed to the correct form. Rimfire pins must be made so that they are not long enough to strike the edge of the chamber, but long enough to fire the cartridge.

Too long a firing-pin will burr or dent the edge of the chamber which results in one of two things. If the burr extends too far into the chamber, it will prevent the empty case from being extracted from the chamber, or if the dents are too deep after the burr has been removed by the judicious use of the file, the rim of the case will not have sufficient support for the pin to fire the cartridge. If this happens, a new cylinder is needed.

Misfires can also be caused by revolvers being out of time —that is, the hand or lever will not push the cylinder into proper alignment with the barrel. This requires lengthening of the hand or lever enough to move the cylinder into proper position. If the hand is so long that it pushes the cylinder beyond the proper position, it must be shortened or adjusted so that when the revolver is fully cocked, the cylinder bolt will lock the cylinder and the barrel in correct alignment.

There are some higher-grade models adaptable more or less to the same type of repair. The hand is usually a part which is relatively easy to make out of a piece of tool-steel or ground stock. The easiest way to make these parts is to soft-solder the original part in place on top of the flat stock, file around it and drill the hole. Usually the old sear is worn off on the tip-end which engages the hammer, and when making a new part, this point is left in the original shape. When finished, new and old parts are separated with a little heat. The new part must be hardened and tempered and this can be done by bringing to red heat and quenching in oil or water, depending on the steel used.

If the type of steel is unknown, such as a piece of scrap or a piece of unidentified steel, it is a good idea to try first tempering a sample piece to see if it is oil-hardening or water-hardening metal. Take a sample piece and heat it cherry red and quench it in oil. If it does not harden try again, quenching it in water. If it does not harden properly then, probably it will not harden by either method and should be discarded. But practice should continue until the amateur has some idea of the best method of hardening and tempering the metal.

An easy way to temper parts of this kind is to put them

on a flat piece of copper and play the torch around an area a little larger than the part being tempered, applying the heat to the bottom side of the plate. The heat will be conducted to the part, which must be closely watched. When the part reaches a straw color, the part must be dropped off into the oil or water.

4. Trigger pulls. There is not much that can be done with the trigger pull on these cheap revolvers. However, some experimenting may get them to work.

The Harrington and Richardson Sportsman was made in the early Thirties and was an excellent gun. If one in good condition can be found it can be regarded as a highly-desirable pistol. A later version of the same Sportsman was made with a solid firing-pin, integral with the hammer, and this never gave much trouble. The H&R Sportsman was a break-open type revolver with a nine-shot cylinder. The action was extremely simple and reliable, and about the only thing that ever happened to them was a broken firing-pin or a broken hand spring.

The Harrington and Richardson Sportsman, not being as rugged as the Colt or Smith and Wesson solid-frame model, may not have stood up under hard usage as well, but when in good condition and well-cared for, was an excellent and desirable gun. They have an extremely good trigger pull that never needs adjustment and the accuracy of the gun was on a par with the world's finest models. This model was made for only a few years and was discontinued at the beginning of World War II.

1. Broken firing-pin. This can be repaired in the same manner as those previously discussed.

2. Broken hand spring. This is merely a straight piece of piano wire and can easily be replaced by a piece of piano wire of the proper diameter cut to the proper length.

There is a companion model known as the Double-Action Sportsman. This was a good gun, but not on a par with the

single-action model. Most of the Single-Action Sportsman revolvers would keep all nine shots inside a dime at fifty feet,
from a machine rest. It is a pity that such a gun was discontinued in favor of guns better classed as Saturday Night Specials.

Semi-Automatic Pistol Problems

1. Magazines fail to lock in place. Many automatic pistols
like the .45 Colt Automatic have some provision for locking
the magazine in place. This is known as the magazine-catch
assembly. If the magazine-catch drags or fails to return to
place, the magazine-catch spring may be broken or the catch
itself become burred somewhere. If the spring is broken; it
must be replaced. If the catch is burred, the burrs may be
removed and smoothed up with a small file. If the catch is
worn excessively it will not retain the magazine in proper
position. When the magazine is locked in position, its bottom
should usually be flush with the butt of the gun. If it protrudes
from the bottom of the gun, the magazine-catch may be worn
and should be replaced.

Sometimes the recess in the magazine which engages the
magazine-catch becomes worn. If this is the trouble, the magazine must be replaced. If the magazine drags excessively as it
is pushed up in the gun, it may be dented. This will cause it
to rub against the side of the frame. If the magazine is excessively dented, it may be necessary to replace it, but some dents
can be removed by inserting a small flat piece of steel inside
the magazine and peening out the dent.

Sometimes the screws holding the grips on an automatic
pistol are too large. This will cause them to interfere with the
magazine as it is being pushed into place. Screws can be shortened sufficiently to rectify the trouble.

It is possible for the wood of a pistol grip to become deformed enough to drag on the magazine. This should be
checked if the magazine fails to go into the gun easily.

2. Feeding troubles. Feeding troubles in automatic pistols are mainly caused by the magazines, which are made of metal and can easily become deformed. If the lips of the magazine become deformed, a cartridge will often stand up straight in the frame of the slide, causing the gun to jam. This is caused by the lips of the magazine being worn or bent. Sometimes a judicious amount of bending will help, but usually a new magazine is required to make it right. About the only thing that can be said about repairs for banged-up magazine clips is that the repairs can only be considered a temporary thing. Such magazines should be replaced as soon as possible.

Sometimes a cartridge will jam on the end of the barrel as it is being fed from the magazine into the chamber. This can be caused by a defective extractor which prevents the cartridge from rising up behind the extractor on its way into the barrel. A burr on the extractor hook can also cause this trouble; if so, it can easily be smoothed up with a small file.

Sometimes the ramp which helps guide the cartridge into the chamber becomes rough enough to cause the bullet to stop on its way to the chamber. To correct this, the ramp can be smoothed up with a file or hone.

It is possible that feeding trouble can be caused by a weak recoil spring, the spring having become so weak that it no longer has the power to strip the fresh cartridge out of the magazine and send it into the barrel. This calls for a new recoil spring. W.C. Wolff Company can supply recoil and main-springs for a large variety of automatic pistols.

In the .45 Automatic Colt pistol, which is a short-recoil action, there are lugs on top of the rear end of the barrel which correspond to recesses on top of the slide. As the slide moves to the rear, the link which connects the barrel to the frame of the gun lowers the barrel out of the locking recess which also slides on to the rear. In the preliminary part of the action (as the slide starts rearward from the action of the barrel) the barrel and slide are locked together and as they start rearward, they travel together. The link disengages the barrel from the slide after the assembly has traveled back about one-quarter inch or so. As the slide returns into a locked position, the link again raises the barrel to lock the barrel and slide together. This is a rather slam-bang action and in time can cause the lugs and top of the barrel to become burred to a point where they will no longer engage the slide.

3. Jams. These burrs will prevent the gun from completely closing and thus prevent it from firing. The recesses in the slide and the lugs on the barrel should be carefully inspected and all burrs removed.

The slide sometimes becomes sufficiently deformed to bind or make the slide action sluggish. This will cause jams since the slide moves too slowly to feed the cartridge into the barrel. By using a very fine file, the slide can be smoothed up enough to allow it to work freely.

4. Extraction troubles. Extraction troubles can be caused by a rough or pitted chamber. Sometimes the chamber can be polished to eliminate this type of extraction trouble, but often this requires the replacement of the barrel, which must be done by a gunsmith.

5. Misfires. The chambers of .22 automatic pistols often become burred by dry-firing, especially in a gun in which the firing-pin is too long or long enough to strike the end of the barrel. This can cause misfires as well as extraction troubles. Often after the burr has been removed, the pit will still be too deep to support the cartridge so that it will not be fired by the firing-pin. This requires replacement of the barrel or at least rebushing the chamber. This would have to be done by a competent gunsmith.

CHAPTER **10**

Making Good Guns Last a Lifetime

A GOOD GUN (and you should never own any other) is made to last a lifetime, and it will if you give it a chance. Some guns are ruined by misuse and neglect. A gun used to press down a barbed wire strand when you climb a fence, or one that is set in a corner where it is pretty sure to get knocked down, or thrown into the back seat to tumble around with the tire chains, will soon begin to look like Junior's popgun, and one put away without oiling will soon cease to bring home the deer or the quail. Knocking a double-barrel shotgun open across your knee and then slamming it shut again, will soon loosen the finest gun. And flinging out a six-gun's cylinder and then snapping it closed with a satisfying click will soon wreck its finely-balanced mechanism.

Always transport your gun in a good case. There are many good cases made and reliable manufacturers make sure that the material used will not be of a kind to encourage sweating and rusting. Sheepskin linings for gun cases have sometimes secured an unwarranted reputation for rusting a gun. This was due to the fact that chemically-tanned sheepskin was some-times used. Oak-tanned skins will not cause sweating.

Between hunting trips, it is all right to keep your gun in a good case if you are sure that your gun is absolutely dry when you put it away—and are also sure that the case is absolutely dry. But a lot of owners like to keep their guns in a good cabinet where they can look at them. The cabinet should be well-ventilated and is best kept locked to prevent people from needlessly handling the guns, as well as to keep any children away from them. I have found that my guns need some kind of muzzle-cap to keep out nest-making mudwasps, who can crawl through an incredibly small ventilating hole. If a scope is mounted on your gun, keep the scope caps in place to protect the lens from dust.

You can buy cabinets from a large number of manufactur-ers. Gray's Gun Shop will supply cabinets in a variety of styles and woods. Coladonato Brothers will supply either cabinets or plans for building them.

Pistols may be kept in a good holster if you wish. All reliable manufacturers take care that their holsters are made out of good material which will not cause sweating.

Guns to be used in cold weather should have all working parts thoroughly cleaned of all oil, and all moving parts should be lubricated with powdered graphite or other powdered lubri-cant.

A gun should never be taken directly from the outdoor cold into a warm room, for this will cause moisture to con-dense on the gun with resultant rusting. It will also cause condensation of the moisture in telescopes, which will fog the lens and possibly rust the telescope adjustments. Arctic hunt-ers usually leave their guns ouside a heated room or cabin. Of course they will not rust while the moisture is frozen.

Most modern guns come with a plastic or varnished stock because this finish can be put on quickly. However, with use this finish is apt to become quickly chipped or marred. About all that can be done with these is to wipe them now and then with a good furniture polish. The best finish for a gun is an oiled finish, for then it can be rubbed with a light coat of linseed oil and polished. Then every time it is rubbed over, it becomes more beautiful.

Cleaning Rifles

The everyday care you will need to give your gun depends on the part of the country in which you live and where you do your hunting. In desert country there is a lot less chance of rusting than there is on the Coast.

A lot is said about guns fired with modern ammunition never needing to be cleaned. It is true that modern ammunition has done away with a great deal of the barrel fouling that used to occur. But we must still contend with moisture from the air and that deposited by the perspiration on our hands. To clean a rifle that has been used only with non-corrosive primers, first push a dry patch through the bore, then a bristle brush saturated with a powder solvent or an all-purpose oil. If the rifle is to be used again shortly, this is all that is necessary. But if it is to be put away for some time, the bore should be protected with a gun grease. A lever-action gun is cleaned in the same way except that it must be cleaned from the muzzle, and care must be taken that the lands are not injured as the rod is pushed in. Hence always use the cleaning rod from the breech end when you can.

The outside of the gun should be carefully wiped with an oiled patch, taking care not to use an excess of oil, and paying special attention to the removal of all fingerprints for these have saline qualities harmful to the metal. It is a good idea to set the gun in the rack with the muzzle down, so that any excess oil may drain off. The gun's chamber should be wiped out regularly, so that oil will not accumulate here, because oil in the chamber greatly increases pressure and can lead to a dangerous situation.

If the gun has become wet, it must be carefully dried. All

salt water spray must be washed from both metal and wood, and these parts oiled. If water has soaked into the wood, the barrel and action must be removed from the wood, and all parts thoroughly dried.

Today all commercial ammunition is loaded with non-corrosive primers. However, many shooters are using .30-06 military ammunition that was loaded with primers containing potassium chlorate. Many handloaders are buying and using those primers because they are cheap. Recently, a customer brought in some such cartridges which he had bought from a regular gun dealer. These were just made up from military cartridges in which the old primers had been left in. If there is any chance that any of these primers have been used in your gun, all traces of the salt must be removed from the gun with water. Fill a can with boiling water. Place the muzzle of the gun in the water, and with a close-fitting rod and flannel patch, pump the water back and forth through the barrel. Then run two or three dry patches through the barrel. This will thoroughly dry the barrel as it will have become quite hot from the hot water. Next push a lightly-oiled patch through the barrel.

Metal fouling is not too common today in the larger calibers, but it is quite common in smallbore high-power rifles, especially in the subcalibers like the .17. This is largely because bullets have not yet been developed for the high speed which these calibers attain. However, metal fouling does occur in almost any caliber rifle, and when it does occur, accuracy is badly off until the metal fouling is relieved.

To make a metal-fouling solution, one that gets rid of such fouling, mix in a large glass bottle:

1 oz. Ammonium persulphate
200 gr. Ammonium carbonate
4 oz. Water

6 oz. Stronger ammonia (available at all
drug stores)

To use the solution, first plug the barrel with a cork. Fill
the barrel completely full of the solution. Be careful not to get
any of the solution on the outside of the barrel as it might
injure the bluing. Allow it to set for about twenty minutes,
then pour it out. After the metal fouling has been removed,
the inside of the gun is still not protected from rust. Pour a
little boiling water through the barrel to dissolve any chemical
left. Then after the barrel is completely dry it should be lightly
oiled.

About once a year an action should be removed from the
stock, cleaned and relubricated. Care should be taken not to
oil it too heavily, as this oil becomes gummy and the action
will become sluggish. If too much oil has been used and allowed to become gummy, the gun will have to be dismantled
and again given a thorough cleaning.

Remove the stock and forearm. Take all moving parts from
the action—such as extractor, cocking cam or levers, etc.
Remove all springs carefully so as not to stretch any coils.

Fill a pan or small container with enough water to completely cover all the parts. If the barrel cannot be easily
removed, immerse only the receiver, allowing the barrel to
project over the edge. Small parts may be wired together for
ease of handling. Add to the water enough Oakite or lye or
similar commercial cleaner to make a strong solution. Allow
to boil until all traces of oil and grease are removed. Add water
when necessary to keep all the parts covered. When the parts
appear perfectly clean, remove them with pliers, shaking to
free them from excess water. While still hot, plunge them into
a pan of light oil.

All small parts and springs should be cleaned with solvent
such as benzine or kerosene. Apply a fine grade of gun oil to
all parts by means of a small paint brush and reassemble.

Shotgun Cleaning

For cleaning a shotgun a jointed wooden rod with brass brushes for the various gauges, felt balls, etc., should be used. Place in the rod, either through the hole, or over the felt ball, a cleaning patch saturated with a good gun oil, and run through the barrel. If the barrel does not appear clean, run through it with the brass brush and again with an oiled patch. Wipe the outside lightly with an oiled patch to remove any moisture or fingerprints on the outside.

New shotgun barrels sometimes accumulate lead. This can usually be removed by cleaning with the brass brush. If leading persists, a little mercuric ointment on a patch run through the barrel will clean it up. This leading is caused by roughness in the barrel and usually smooths up after the gun has been shot a few times. If it persists, the barrel may be lapped by a gunsmith.

Revolver Maintenance

Revolvers are cleaned in much the same manner as the rifle, but special attention must be given to the chambers and the cylinder ratchets. Partly-burned powder under the revolver's extractor or up front where the crane should swing tightly against the frame, can prevent proper locking of the cylinder, therefore this should be carefully cleaned. The cylinder ratchets also should be cleaned and covered with a light coat of oil.

Likewise the breech face on a .22 automatic must be kept free of caked grease which can hold the extractor too far out to extract properly.

Using Touch-Up Blue

There are a number of cold blues which are suitable for touch-up when a spot becomes worn or a scratch on the blue is found. All of these preparations are extremely easy to use, but the one that comes in paste form is becoming the most popular. One of the best is the Birchwood Perma-Blu. The directions for its use are printed on the package and these directions are always simple. The same company also furnishes several other very good products of interest to the gun buff. Especially noteworthy are their stock-finishing kits and powder solvents. Another excellent cold blue and one that is very easy to use, is known as Formula 44-40, manufactured by Numrich Arms Co.

CHAPTER **11**

Removing Barrel Obstructions

THE EASIEST WAY to correct a mistake is not to make it. The easiest way to handle the problem of an obstruction in a barrel is not to get an obstruction in it in the first place. However, obstructions are often found in a rifle, shotgun or pistol barrel. Sometimes they are caused by carelessness, sometimes by some reason beyond the shooter's control.

If you like to carry ammunition loose in a trouser or coat pocket, it is well to mix no other objects in with the ammunition for gunsmiths will testify that shooters sometimes jam into their guns such objects as loose buttons or coins. The shooter must always be on the lookout to detect and remove simple obstructions such as mud or snow. And shotgunners who like to use handloads must always be on guard against using the same shell cases too many times for reloading. Otherwise they invite undue possibility of case separation, for firing another round in a barrel in which part of a shell casing has already stuck may result in a bad accident or a ruined gun barrel.

Bullet Stuck in Barrel

One of the most common rifle barrel obstructions is a bullet lodged in the barrel. There are several ways in which this might happen. Sometimes a handloader forgets to put powder in the cartridge, and when the powderless cartridge is fired, the primer has sufficient power to drive the bullet into the bore where it stops. Sometimes a loaded cartridge is extracted from the chamber but leaves the bullet in the barrel.

When a rifle barrel is chambered, a short section of the rifling is reamed out just forward of the chamber. This is often referred to as the throat of the chamber. If this is too short, the bullet may be caught in the barrel. Or the bullet may not be seated deeply enough in the cartridge case. Either condition might lead to a swollen chamber or a blown-up action.

Sometimes old military ammunition lacks the power to push the bullet all the way out of the barrel. The shooter, not realizing this, fires another bullet behind the first one lodged in the barrel, causing a blow-up. Sometimes this happens in revolvers, the first bullet going partly out of the barrel, then another is fired behind this and still another behind this. This results in giving the barrel a sort of corduroy appearance, but does not necessarily result in a blown-up gun because enough gas escapes from between the cylinder and the end of the barrel to lower the pressure enough to prevent complete rupture of the barrel.

In a revolver, where length of bore is not great, the bullet can be driven out by using a smooth rod which fits the bore rather closely. A bullet in a rifle throat can be pushed out in this same way. A bullet lodged further in the barrel—about midway between the breech and the muzzle—presents more of a problem. Sometimes it can be driven out by using a polished drill rod and a heavy hammer; sometimes it cannot be budged. When the bullet is so tightly lodged that it cannot be moved, it is often necessary to use a drill attached to the proper-sized rod. This kind of obstruction problem cannot usually be solved by an amateur. The safe way is to take it to a competent gunsmith.

The most important thing to remember about a bullet lodged in a rifle barrel is *never fire another bullet behind the lodged one!* If you do, invariably the action or the barrel will suffer serious damage, to say nothing of the liklihood of serious danger to the shooter, himself.

Cleaning Patch Lodged In Barrel

Another common obstruction is caused by a cleaning patch being too tight or coming off inside the bore while being pushed back and forth by the rod. Sometimes a few drops of oil allowed to soak into the patch will permit it to be pushed out with a close-fitting rod. If this does not work, a special tool can be made by soldering a wood screw to a rod. Both screw and rod should be very close to the diameter of the bore. The head of the screw should be cut off and the screw attached to the rod, preferably by silver-soldering. Such a special tool is called a "worm." It is inserted into the barrel and turned so that the screw engages the stuck patch, then the screw and the patch can be pulled out together. Sometimes, in spite of everything, the stuck patch will persist in sticking. When it is known positively that the obstruction is only a patch, the

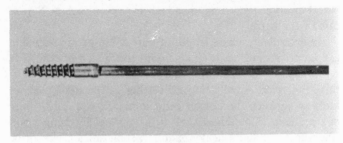

A screw attached to a rod for the removal of obstructions in the barrel.

barrel can be heated to a point where it will melt soft solder. This amount of heat will in no way harm the barrel or the bluing, but it will char the patch to a point where it can easily be pushed out by a rod.

Removing Unknown Obstructions

One of the most serious problems confronting the gun owner is trying to remove a barrel obstruction of unknown character. For example, a hunter accidentally gets something in his gun barrel. This could be a bullet as described before. If he is in the woods or field away from any tools, he often proceeds to use a piece of wire from a nearby fence, a willow stick, or anything that will enter the bore. Inevitably this conglomeration of tools finds its way into the barrel to a point completely obstructing it. Often the green twig, such as the willow switch, contains a high percentage of water and, if not removed soon, the barrel will rust. Here again heat is the only solution. A reasonable amount of heat (enough to melt solder) will dry out the green twig enough to where it may fall out of the barrel of its own accord. Then, once this type of material has been removed from the bore, the bullet can usually be poked out with a good rod.

One of the hardest obstructions to remove is a piece of copper tubing or a soft cleaning rod which, when pounded against the obstruction, has expanded to a point where it has almost become a part of the barrel itself and any further pounding will merely expand it more. Sometimes oil can be poured into the barrel and allowed to flow around the obstruction so that a steady pressure on a good stiff rod, of a size close to that of the bore, may move it. Sometimes the only solution is to replace the barrel.

When mentioning a rod suitable for removing obstructions, it is usually referred to as a "close-fitting rod," and this size is very important. The best kind is a piece of polished drill rod, which is obtainable at some hardware stores or at all wholesale hardware supply houses. Large supply houses carry drill rod in fractional sizes by sixty-fourths, making it possible for anyone to purchase a rod which will nearly fit any bore. For example, if a rod is to be used in a .30 caliber barrel, a 9/32 in. rod will work fine since it is only a few thousandths smaller than the .30 caliber bore. Or if a closer fit is needed, a 19/64 in. drill rod will just slide through the .30 caliber barrel. In a case like this, it may enter the bore for a few inches and then "seize," and will itself become an almost irresistible obstruction, welding itself to the walls of the bore so that even if it is driven out, it will ruin the bore. For a .25 caliber bore, a 15/64 in. drill rod is about right; for a .22 bore, a 3/16 in. rod will work; for a .270, a 17/64 in.; and for a .35, 21/64 in.

Sometimes a broken shell constitutes a chamber or barrel obstruction. The owner of a rifle which is prone to this trouble should obtain a "broken-shell extractor" for his rifle. These gadgets are relatively inexpensive and remove broken shells with the least amount of trouble. In the absence of a broken-shell extractor, a rod in one of the above mentioned sizes— which will slide through the neck of the broken case—can be filed to a shape where it can be used to remove a broken case. A sort of mushroom head should be filed on the end of this rod, then this head is split for about one inch with a hacksaw.- The two halves are finally bent apart with a screwdriver so

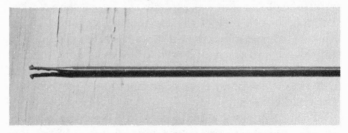

Improvised "broken-shell extractor." The notches are first filed on the rod, then the rod is split with a hacksaw and wedged open.

that they will expand to a diameter slightly larger than the inside diameter of the case-neck. From the breech end of the barrel this expanded portion can then be pushed through the neck of the case, whereupon it will spring back to size and catch or grip the end of the broken neck. Then a rod through the muzzle-end of the barrel can be used to push both this tool and the broken case out of the chamber.

Sometimes a case can be removed by using a round file, one just large enough to contact the broken case somewhere along its inner walls. The file can be pushed and sort of screwed into the broken case until it "bites" into the brass. Then the broken case will sometimes pull out with the file. There are other alternatives. Sometimes it is possible to find a thread tap of the proper size so that it can be threaded into the neck of the broken case, or a tap can be found that will bite into the brass without touching the bore, so that the case can be snagged out with the tap.

One of the surest ways to ruin a barrel is to try to remove a broken case by inserting an ice pick or some other sharp tool between the brass case and the chamber, in an effort to pry the two apart. This almost always ruins the chamber.

Sometimes case separations are caused by an overload, the fired case expanding so tightly into the chamber that no type of broken-shell extractor will remove it. In such a case, it is necessary to take the gun to a competent gunsmith.

The trick with any of these methods is to always be sure that the wall of the chamber is never damaged by contact with a tool.

CHAPTER 12

About
Soldering

SOFT SOLDERING and silver soldering are an essential part of
gun work. Front sight ramps, rear sight bases and other attachments can be very satisfactorily and permanently attached
by soft soldering. Usually this can be accomplished by the use
of a butane torch, an ordinary gasoline blow torch, or the
Prest-O-Lite torch. Sometimes a soldering iron (copper) is
useful, but most of the ordinary soldering requirements pertaining to gun work can be best accomplished with any of the
above torches.

Soft Soldering

To attach a sight ramp by means of soft soldering, the first
requirement is to thoroughly clean the two parts to be joined.
For example, most of the ramps on the market are furnished
blued. The bluing must be removed from the underside of the
ramp. This can be done by using a piece of emery cloth on
a round file, or in some instances by the round file itself. Any

method to thoroughly remove and clean the underside of the ramp can be used. The ramp is then placed in the correct location on the barrel and outlined with an ordinary lead pencil. Usually such a mark is sufficiently visible so that the bluing on the barrel can be completely removed just inside the lines. The reason for not removing the old finish completely out to the lines is to prevent leaving bright areas around the ramp which would thereby require a rebluing job. When both pieces have been thoroughly cleaned, each must be thoroughly tinned (coated with solder). One of the best sources of supply for silver solder is Handy and Harmon, El Monte, Calif. The material comes in ribbon or round type. The same company also furnishes silver-solder flux. The best solder to use is just plain half-and-half solder wire. Acid-core wire solder can be used, but it often injures the bluing on the surrounding areas.

The ideal flux is that sold by either Montgomery Ward or Sears Roebuck. This is the liquid type and is relatively non-corrosive; that is, everything in the vicinity will not rust from the fumes of this kind of flux. Some liquid-solder fluxes, when vaporized from the heat, induce rust on any steel surfaces exposed throughout the room. To properly tin the polished areas, heat the areas (using a torch) to a temperature where the solder will start to melt, using a piece of wire solder. The work can be checked from time to time as the heating proceeds. Once the parts will melt solder, or are hot enough to almost melt it, use a swab that has been dampened in the soldering fluid. Where the parts are to be blued, the swab can simply be dipped into the flux since a surplus of fluid will do no harm. But where the surrounding surfaces are not to be refinished, then it is necessary to use the flux sparingly. An excellent method for applying the flux is to simply use a small mucilage brush, but in the absence of this kind of a tool, a swab can easily be made by wrapping a cleaning patch around the end of a piece of baling wire or a small stick like a lollypop stick, and tying it in place. As soon as the solder starts to melt, use a swab to spread the molten solder over all of the area to be joined. A very thin coat is all that is needed, but it must *completely* cover the surfaces to be joined. With a little practice this operation will be found very simple to accomplish. Before doing a job on a fine rifle, it is advisable, of course, to practice on something that has no value.

When the two surfaces to be joined have been thoroughly tinned and any excess solder wiped off leaving the surfaces perfectly plated with solder, allow them to cool to a point where they can be handled. Then set the barreled action in the vise as described for installing scope blocks or mount bases. Place the ramp in position and, using a parallel clamp and a cross-test level, locate the ramp so that it is level with either the rear sight or the bottom of the action. When the ramp is properly located and tightly clamped in place with the two soldered surfaces together, again heat the barrel and ramp to a point where the solder is easily melted. By holding the piece of wire solder at one end of the ramp, the solder can be fed into the joint as it starts to cool. Many times ramps have a screwhole in them, then the solder can be fed into this hole so that it will flow through the joint. Some bubbles of solder may appear along the edge of the ramp, but these can be wiped off with a dry cloth just before they solidify.

If the parts have been properly cleaned and tinned and the joint thoroughly sweated together, the ramp will be permanently attached to the barrel, and it will withstand rebluing by the salts-immersion process if the joint is tight enough to prevent the bluing solution from working into it.

Often there will be a blemished spot left on the original blue finish after soft-soldering a ramp in place, in spite of utmost care. These small spots can be touched up by using one of the cold-bluing solutions advertised in gun magazines. One of the best is the solution known as 44/40 sold by Numrich Arms, West Hurley, New York.

As a final reminder, when sweating two parts together such as a ramp and barrel, there are three essential requirements: first, parts must be fitted as closely as possible so as to make the thinnest possible joint; secondly, the two surfaces to be joined must be completely and thoroughly tinned; and third, sufficient heat must be used to thoroughly melt the solder yet not discolor the parts. If the heat becomes too great, the parts will oxidize or be heat-blued, which is an indication of too much heat. When the parts become heat-blued, the solder will not stick.

The foregoing description for sweating on front-sight ramps can also be used for sweating scope-mount bases in place, telescope blocks, receiver sight bases, etc. Sometimes a receiver sight base, for example, is an odd shape or has to fit on an odd-shaped surface, where it is very difficult to hold the base in place while drilling. Sometimes a base of this kind can be sweated into position so as to hold it firmly while the holes are being drilled and the screws installed. This makes an excellent job since the solder and screws together pretty well insure that the base will never come loose.

Sometimes receiver sight bases or scope blocks have a tendency to loosen up from heavy recoil, if screws are the only thing holding them in place. Such bases can be tinned and then be reattached in correct position by means of the regular screws and then heat applied in the same manner as described for attaching the ramp. Once the area becomes hot enough to melt solder, the screws can be thoroughly tightened and the assembly allowed to cool. This produces an extra-tight installation which will never again come loose without application of heat.

Sometimes this is also true of improperly attached scope mounts which have a tendency to shear off the attaching screw or to become loose. A small area can be polished and tinned on the underside of each end of the base, and corresponding spots can be polished on the receiver, then the two parts can be sweated together. This will not work, however, on aluminum bases.

Often side-mounted telescope bases, such as the Griffin and Howe and others which are made of steel, can only be held in place by the combination screw-and-sweating method.

It is even possible to sweat into place rifle barrels which have become loose. This sometimes happens with the Model 92 Winchester and other similar models, where the barrel becomes loose to a point where it will be off-center if it is tightened. The threads on both barrel and action should be thoroughly cleaned so that no dirt or grease remains. Then the threads on the barrel can be tinned in the usual manner using the liquid flux. Both receiver and barrel are heated to a point where solder is easily melted. Then a liberal amount of the liquid flux is applied to the threads inside the receiver and the barrel can be screwed back and forth. This will transfer some of the solder to the threads inside the receiver. It is not necessary to have a perfect tinning job in cases of this kind. It is all right as long as there are several spots to which the solder is firmly adhering. Then the two parts are screwed together, being sure that the barrel is in correct position. This can be done with a cross-test level if it is an octagon barrel, or usually, the barrel will be straight enough. If a cross-test level is used on a round barrel, the flat of one of the sight dovetails can be used for a surface on which to rest a level. This makes a permanent repair for the only way the barrel can again be removed is by applying heat.

When the job is finished, the whole assembly should be thoroughly cleaned and oil applied to prevent rust, since the flux has a tendency to induce rust. This means, of course, that any soldering job, when finished, should be protected against rust.

Silver Soldering

The small Prest-O-Lite torch is fine for silver soldering small parts. A butane or propane torch can also be used, but usually not as satisfactorily as the Prest-O-Lite torch. Hardly any of these small torches produce enough heat to satisfactorily silver-solder large parts together, including installing front sight ramps. However, the large tips can be used for silver soldering ramps in place if the inside of the barrel is protected against

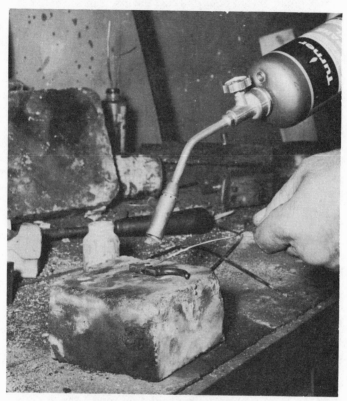

Silver-soldering the trigger after removal of a small section to shorten the part.

scaling. In generating the amount of heat possible with a welding torch, the Prest-O-Lite torch requires more time which in turn induces oxidation inside the barrel causing scale. So it is advantageous to protect the inside of the bore in some manner. A mixture that is sometimes used for this can be made by using one part lamp black, one and one-half parts of ordinary kitchen flour and two parts fine table salt. Mix into a thick liquid or thin paste and coat the inside of the bore near the area to be heated.

Incidentally, this mixture is also recommended for bending files. Many times a curved triangular file is needed for a special job. By coating the straight file with the above mixture, it can be heated to a cherry red and while still hot, be bent to the desired shape, then immediately quenched in water or oil. The protective coating can then be brushed off and the file will be as good as ever.

Getting back to the barrel, however; after the bore has been coated with this mixture, the ramp and barrel are prepared in the same manner as described for the soft-soldering method.

One of the most common and easily used silver solders is known as Easy-Flo 45, produced by Handy & Harmon, 4140 Gibson Road, El Monte, California, 91731. This material is furnished in various sizes, both round and ribbon. For soldering on ramps, ¼ in. ribbon, .002 in. to .003 in. (not over .005 in.) thick works very well, and 1/16 in. wire silver solder is best for repairing many parts where the ribbon type is not practical. With this Easy-Flo solder, the company furnishes Handy Flux, which is made especially for use with this type of silver solder.

To attach a ramp which has been properly prepared, coat the under surface with Handi-Flux, which is sort of a paste, and then lay a strip of ribbon solder on top of the flux, the strip being slightly shorter than the ramp. Apply a light coat of flux to the barrel and then clamp the two parts together in the same manner as described for the soft-soldering method. Once the ramp has been leveled and clamped into position, apply heat as evenly as possible to the sides, top, and bottom of the barrel until the silver solder melts. The barrel will usually turn a very dull red, but this is not hot enough to injure the barrel's original heat treatment. The heat must be applied as evenly as possible to also avoid warping the barrel.

Those who claim that silver-soldering ramps on the muzzle-end of a gun destroys accuracy, fail to take into consideration the fact that most commercial guns have ramps silver-soldered on, and the author, having been a rifle barrel-maker for over thirty years, has attached thousands of ramps in this manner, and gunsmiths all over the country use the method with 100% success. This, of course, assumes use of the right type of silver solder and technique. It can easily be imagined how easy it is to ruin a barrel if all the heat is applied quickly to the bottom of the barrel. The top will be cool, while the bottom is heated. This will result in a kink. But just because this can and does happen, is no reason for condemning the practice, in general.

When the proper temperature is reached, the flux begins to melt and will come out from between the two parts as a sort of glassy-appearing liquid. When this occurs, it is necessary to keep the heat up for only a minute or so and then allow it to cool. A little practice is required, it being best to practice on two pieces of metal approximately the same size as the actual gun parts.

A properly silver-soldered joint is almost as strong as a welded one and is not weakened by any bluing solution. But since it requires considerable amounts of heat, the parts almost always have to be reblued.

Often broken parts can be permanently repaired by the silver-soldering method, unless such parts must be again heat-treated. But any parts such as a broken trigger or something like that, can be thus permanently repaired very easily.

CHAPTER 13

Installing
New Sights
and Mounts

SIGHTS, telescope mounts and telescope blocks can be put on
a gun very satisfactorily, using extremely simple methods and
a minimum of equipment.

Attaching Sights, Mounts, Etc.

Most rifles of current manufacture and many of the previous
models are already drilled and tapped for telescope mounts,
bases and receiver sights, with the holes plugged with dummy
screws. All you need to do here is to remove the plug screws
and install the sight with the screws that accompany it.

The spacing of holes for the micrometer rear sight and
telescope mounts and blocks is standard for almost any sight,
and inexpensive jigs are available for drilling the more common actions such as the Springfield, Enfield, and Mauser from
C.R. Pederson & Son and B-Square Engineering Co. When
using these jigs, the only critical adjustment is to locate the

holes so that the sight base will not interfere with the operation of the bolt handle. Nearly all receiver sights for bolt-
action rifles are located either on the left or right side of the
bridge, rather than on top.

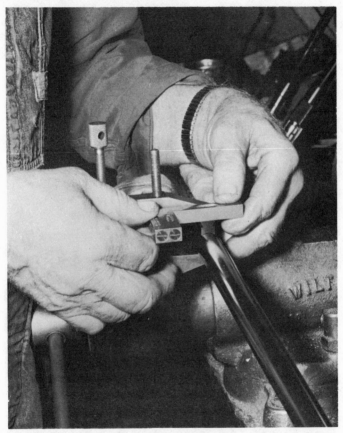

Positioning telescope *blocks,* using a cross-test level and parallel clamps.

However, the average amateur would not have enough use
for a jig to make it worth going to the expense of buying one.

In the absence of a jig, micrometer rear sights and scope mounts such as Redfield, Buehler, or similar top mounts can be accurately located and securely held in place by parallel clamps while you make the holes for the mounting screws.

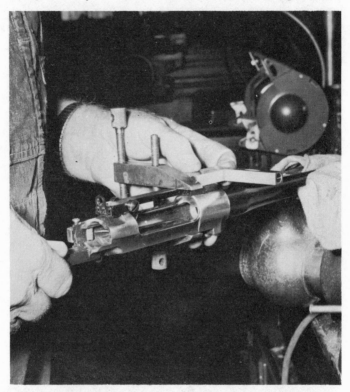

Positioning scope *mount* by using cross-test level and parallel clamps.

To easily and accurately locate the mount or sight base, first remove the barreled-action from the stock; remove the bolt in a bolt-action, and it may be necessary to remove the trigger. Clamp the barrel in the vise, using some means of protection for the barrel such as wood or leather-lined jaws, or in the absence of anything better, the barrel can simply be well wrapped in a rag so the vice jaws won't scar it. It does not have to be held very tightly for this operation.

Level the action by means of a cross-test level. The small cross-test level is one of the most useful tools because it has the form of a small square, which makes its application quite universal. It is relatively inexpensive, costing only $2 or $3, and the catalog designation is Cross Test Level and Plumb #134. Everyone interested in fine tools, especially those to be used in the gunshop, should procure the latest Starrett catalog. This is free for the asking either from L.S. Starrett Co. or from any distributor carrying Starrett tools. Besides describing Starrett products, it is an excellent handbook, containing tables such as tap drill sizes, decimal equivalents, etc. Another good tool catalog is one from Brown & Sharp Manufacturing Co.

For most bolt-actions, the leveling can be done across the bottom of the action. In the case of lever-actions and some other types, the cross-test level can be used on the receiver's flat side with the level's cross-arm extending over the top of the action. When the action is level, both longitudinally and crosswise, fasten the mount or sight base in place with a parallel clamp. Be sure to position the mount base as far ahead as possible so that the recoil lug fits solidly against the end of the receiver. This is important because a heavy scope may cause the screws to shear off if this recoil lug is not so arranged that it will absorb most of the recoil in the base rather than on the screws. A micrometer rear sight will ordinarily be located as far back or as near the shooter's eye as possible. Since the action and the barrel have been leveled, a cross-test level can next be used to level the base. The base can be positioned quite accurately by adjusting it while loosening and tightening the clamp. When the base is level with the action, the clamp should be tightened enough to hold the base securely in place.

Almost all American scope mounts, sights and other accessories use the 6-48 screw, the tap drill for which is #31. Sometimes a drill and tap is supplied with the mounts. Before drilling with the #31, select another drill from the wire gauge drill set which fits the screw holes in the mount perfectly. This

A Number 31 drill used for drilling for a telescope block and a receiver sight. Note the piece of tubing slipped over the drill to prevent it from going too deep. The tubing may be soft-soldered to the drill if necessary, or it can be of such length as to act as a spacer between the drill chuck and the work.

latter drill can then be used as a guide drill with which to spot the holes. These spots should be made very shallow, or no larger than can be made with the guide drill without its body beginning to cut. The barreled-action and scope mount assembly can be held in place with V-Blocks on a drill-press base. After making the spotting holes, final holes are then actually drilled to desired depth with the #31 drill.

Remove the assembly from the V-block and tap the holes next, using a 6-48 *carbon steel* tap. Many actions will tap very easily without any annealing or preliminary work. Some alloy-steel actions are very difficult to drill and tap, but it can often be done anyway without annealing by using the proper lubricant. One of the best is ordinary nitro-solvent. For example,

Hoppes' #9 Nitro Solvent contains several excellent tapping lubricants such as sperm oil, turpentine, kerosene, and so forth. This means that the general mixture found in most nitro solvents makes an excellent lubricant for tapping in almost any kind of steel. *The reason for using a carbon-steel tap is that no matter how proficient anyone may become, a tap will now and then be broken.*

If the tap is broken off in a hole which goes all the way through, a stiff punch can be used to drive the broken piece all the way through the hole. This will seldom harm the threads that have been already cut, so the hole can be re-tapped. If the *carbon tap* is broken off in a blind hole, it can be warmed up enough with a torch to anneal it so that it can be drilled out if it cannot be removed any other way. Sometimes a broken tap can be removed with a small punch if it happens to break from wobbling or something like that, but when a tap breaks because of being too tight in a hole, it almost always has to be drilled out. A small tip for the Prest-O-Lite torch can be used to soften the tap broken off in a hole of this kind without harming the receiver—just heat the tap until it is black, but protect the receiver as described for spot-annealing before drilling. Then center-punch the piece of the tap and drill it out with the #31 drill. *Should a high-speed steel tap be used, it cannot be annealed, thus it will be practically impossible to remove if it breaks.*

After the holes have been tapped, the mount base can be left clamped in place while the screws are being installed. With a little practice, one mount base like this can be put on in five or ten minutes this way and the job will be entirely satisfactory.

A necessary precaution, of course, is to make sure that the *rear end* of the base *is perfectly centered.* This is usually more or less automatic, since the underside of the base is contoured, but it should be closely examined to make sure that it is not off-center before you do any drilling.

The same method can be used to install receiver-sight bases. When installing scope-mount bases, receiver-sight bases, etc., receivers are often found which are too hard to tap.

Spot annealing the Springfield C3-A3 receiver, using a large soldering copper. Note the drop of solder between the receiver and the copper, which transmits the heat to the small spot on the receiver.

Some of these receivers will simply have a case-hardened surface. An example of this is the old low-numbered Springfield with a serial number under 800,000. Since the bridge area of a bolt-action is not critical, a small torch can be used to slowly heat the bridge either on the side, for a receiver sight, or on the top for a scope-mount base. Play the torch on the area where the hole will be drilled and slowly heat it until the color turns black; then let it cool.

Using an asbestos dam for spot-annealing a receiver.

In areas like the receiver ring, where strength and the heat treatment is critical, a small mounted point (stone) can sometimes be used in an electric drill to grind a starting spot through the case-hardening, large enough to allow the screw hole to be drilled. If this does not work, then the receiver may be spot-annealed by using a fairly heavy soldering copper. Polish the spot to be annealed ¼ in. or so in diameter, then use the soldering copper which has been previously heated so that it will melt solder instantly. Place the point of the soldering copper on the center of the spot to be annealed. Use a drop of soldering fluid such as the product sold by Handy & Harmon, Sears Roebuck, or Montgomery Ward. Then melt a drop of solder by contacting it with the point of the soldering copper. This will immediately form a bubble of solder around the point which will spread over the polished spot as the heat is transmitted from the copper to the steel. Hold this in position for several minutes until the solder is just barely in molten condition, then it can simply be wiped off with a cloth. This will usually anneal the receiver in the small spot which was covered by the solder; in turn, this can then be drilled. Usually a carbon steel drill is all right, but a high-speed drill sometimes does a better job. Another way to spot-anneal a receiver is to build up a small dam of asbestos, leaving the center (¼ in. diameter) bare. Then the Prest-O-Lite torch can be used to heat the spot in the center of the asbestos until it becomes black.

Taps come in three styles: starting-taps—which have a long taper in order to facilitate the starting of the tap in the hole; a plug-tap which has a more blunt point; and a bottoming-tap which is almost flat on the end in order to cut threads all the way to the bottom of a blind hole. Only the plug-type tap will be needed.

One of the best sources of supply of 6-48 taps is the Lyman Gun Sight Corporation, Middlefield, Connecticut. They can also furnish #31 drills to go with these taps.

For gun work, a plug-tap will start satisfactorily without the use of a starting-tap and for a bottoming-tap one of the

Drilling for Redfield mount with the electric drill placed in the drill press attachment. The position of the mount set up in the parallel clamps.

plug-types can be ground off to eliminate most of the lead. Sometimes a hole will be very difficult to tap. The tap will have a tendency to stick in the hole and squeak, indicating that the metal is almost on the verge of being too hard to tap. Often this trouble can be solved by re-grinding the tap with very,

Center drilling for telescope blocks with a hand drill.

very little lead to a degree almost equal to that of a bottoming-tap. It is surprising how much better a tap ground in this manner will cut hard metal as compared to one with a greater lead. This is one of the small tricks that is often described as a trade secret.

In the absence of the small drill press attachment referred to elsewhere, holes for the mounting screws can be drilled directly into the barrel using an electric drill, being careful to keep the drill as straight as possible and also checking the work carefully to make sure that the hole is not drilled too deep. The same operation can be accomplished using an ordinary hand drill. To keep from drilling the hole too deep, a piece of tubing can be placed on the drill to act as a stop (see illustration).

Sometimes the shape of a receiver is such that a parallel clamp will not hold the sight base well. In such instances an ordinary C-clamp can often be used, or a C-clamp can sometimes be modified for a particular job. C-clamps are relatively inexpensive and can be obtained in almost any hardware or department store. When there is no way to hold a sight base in position so it can serve as a guide for drilling, a small center-punch can be made with a point which will fit the holes in the base perfectly. The base can then be held in place by hand and leveled, using the cross-test level while this center-punch is being held in place simply by slipping it into one of the holes in the base. When the sight base is satisfactorily positioned, a light tap with a hammer on this special center-punch will well-enough mark the hole so that after the sight base has been removed, a regular center-punch can be used to deepen the mark for drilling. Then, this first hole can be tapped and the sight base attached as tightly as possible using only the one screw. The base can then be aligned properly through using the cross-test level and the second hole drilled, using the base as a guide. Scope blocks can be mounted in the same manner as described for a scope-mount base. The rear block is long enough so that the parallel clamp can be positioned in the center of the block, leaving the two holes open for drilling.

The cross-test level is invaluable for this kind of work.

Once the rear block has been attached so that it is relatively square with the action, the front block can be positioned 7.2 in. forward of the rear blocks, the measurement being taken center-to-center of the two blocks. Sometimes 6 in. center-to-center is used, or some other measurement may be used under special circumstances, but a block spacing of 7.2 in. will permit minute-of-angle adjustments on the telescope mounts. Any other spacing will give more-or-less "random" sight adjustments, unsatisfactory to most shooters.

So far we've been discussing mounting mainly the rear block or base. The front block, now, is positioned in the same manner as described for the rear block, the rear block now being used as a base for the level so as to position the front block perfectly level with the rear one. Since the parallel clamp will cover one of the holes in the short, front block, the first —perferably the forward hole—can be drilled and tapped, and its screw inserted and tightened down as tightly as possible, which will allow the clamp to be removed. Then the rear hole can be drilled, using the hole in the base as a guide, as previously described for other mount bases.

Sometimes the receiver is of such awkward shape that it is impossible to clamp the sight base in place. If care is taken, a center-punch fitting the hole in the base can be placed in the hole and the base held in place by hand. Level with the cross-test level to correspond with some flat surface on the receiver which is perpendicular to the bore, then the punch, already placed in the hole, can be lightly tapped with a small hammer. This makes a mark for one hole. When this hole has been drilled and tapped, the sight can be attached in position through this hole and the other one made.

On the pessimistic side, if, through carelessness, the sight proves to be cockeyed, or slightly out of line, sometimes the sight base can be shimmed to straighten it up. But if it is so bad that even shimming will not correct the condition, the holes can sometimes be drilled out to a larger size such as the

10-32, and a 10-32 screw put into the hole flush with the bottom, or down as far as possible in a blind hole. First, however, the hole should be fluxed and tinned with soft solder, then the screw, with a drop of flux on it, can be turned into the hole while the solder is still molten, and by turning the screw back and forth, the screw itself will become coated with solder. Then, by keeping the area warm enough to keep the solder melted, the screw can be turned into the correct position. Next, when the work is cool enough to handle, the screw can be cut off with a file, flush with the receiver. Finally, the hole for the sight can now be redrilled and tapped.

Another way often observed is to simply move the sight to a new position, moving it as little as possible, then doing the drilling and tapping again in the new position, using plug screws for the old holes. However, sometimes there is not room enough to move the sight or mount base to make room for such new holes, and in this case it is necessary to plug the original hole as already described.

Making Dovetails

Often it becomes necessary to install open sights on rifle barrels which have not been dovetailed. Where the dovetail is already in the barrel, a soft copper punch is best for driving out the old sights (which always drive out from left to right, and drive in from right to left). In order to remove dovetail sights, which are often quite tight, the barrel must be held securely in the vise, using wood or leather-lined jaws. If these are not available, the barrel may be wrapped in a rag to protect it.

When a new dovetail must be cut, it can be done with an ordinary triangular file. One side of this file should first be ground smooth, that is, the teeth are completely ground off one surface, which creates what is called a safe-side file. The barrel must be clamped in the vise, and the receiver or some point that is square must be checked with the cross-test level. The dovetail to be cut must be properly located according to the gun owner's wishes, then it can be partially cut, using a hacksaw, making sure that the hacksaw cuts are neither too deep nor too wide. Using the safe-side file, next rough out the dovetail, making its bottom as flat as possible, checking from time to time with a cross-test level. Care must be taken to shape the dovetail relatively square with the axis of the barrel. Whether it is a front or a long open rear sight to be driven into the finished dovetail, it must be relatively parallel to the barrel. In cutting a slot of this kind, the safe-side on the file allows the dovetail to be widened without simultaneously deepening it. The safe-side also allows the corners of the dovetail to be filed sharp. By contrast, the corner of an ordinary file is quite round, and it will not cut the sharp corner needed in the dovetail. A little practice with a safe-side file will enable almost any fair mechanic to make fairly-satisfactory dovetail cuts. Make the dovetail slots .090 in. deep.

CHAPTER 14

Putting on Recoil Pads Is Easy

THE INSTALLATION of a recoil pad is the same for either a rifle or a shotgun. When installing a pad on a new stock which has not been finished, the pad can simply be installed on the butt with the two screws furnished with the pad, or with the two screws plus some kind of cement. Contact cement, DuPont Household Cement, or some kind of glue works very well. Cementing the pad on is not necessary, but it will help correct any imperfect contact between the wood and the pad. However, a pad installed on a stock which is held in place by a draw-bolt or a through-bolt, should never be cemented on since, in order to remove the stock, the pad would first have to be removed to allow unscrewing the bolt. When attaching the pad to a completely finished stock, especially on a new gun, great care must be taken not to harm the original finish.

Making Your Stock Fit You

When attaching a butt plate, it is possible for a shooter to alter his stock so that it will fit him better. In shotguns, particularly, fit is very important, because here the hunter does not have

A simple way to measure pitch is to clamp or rivet a straightedge to the long side of a two-foot square, making sure that the straightedge is clamped perfectly parallel to the inside. The butt of the gun is placed on the short end of the square with both toe and heel touching the square and the rear end of the sighting plane touching the vertical edge. The pitch is measured as shown. The gun in the illustration has about 2.5 in. down pitch. If the front sight should touch the upright, it would indicate that the gun has no pitch.

The pitch can also be measured by using a wall instead of the upright.

time to sight the gun, but must hurry it to his shoulder and fire. If it fits him, he has only to draw it to his shoulder in a natural position and fire. One old-timer described this situation by saying that if a shotgun fits, all the shooter has to do is to keep his eye on the bird and the gun will take care of itself. If it does not fit, *he must* take *aim* and by the time he has done this, the bird is gone.

To have proper fit, the comb must be of the right height and thickness, and the drop at the stock's heel must be correct for the shooter. Much of this will depend on his build and manner of shooting.

The "pull" is the distance from the center of the trigger to the center of the butt plate. The length of pull is right when the stock is short enough so that it does not get tangled in the shooter's clothing or hang up on his shoulder. (Be sure to take into account the extra clothing usually worn hunting.) It is long enough when the shooter's right thumb does not bump into his nose.

The comb should be high enough so that when the shooter's cheek rests naturally on the stock, his eye will be in the line of sight along the barrel. A high comb causes the shooter to shoot up, since it places his eye above the front sight of the gun. Thus, if you are shooting birds, or at a rapidly rising target, a slightly higher comb is an advantage.

All drop and pitch measurements are made from the line of sight. Pitch can be measured by simply standing the gun against a vertical wall, with the butt touching the floor at both heel and toe, and the breech of the gun—or the rear sight, as the case may be—touching the wall. The pitch is the distance between the muzzle or the front sight and the wall. The amount of drop desired is largely dependent on the shooter's build. A man with square shoulders and a long neck can use a very straight stock, while a man with a short neck requires more drop. A straighter stock has the advantage of bringing the recoil straight back to the shooter's shoulder, and so makes the kick less noticeable. If there is too little pitch, there is a tendency for the gun to slip down and then the barrel will point up; if there is too much pitch, the gun will slip up on the shoulder and the barrel will point down. Between two- and three-inches down-pitch is common.

Cutting the Stock to Length

The first step in installing a recoil pad is to cut the butt stock to the proper length. If the length of pull is correct before the pad is installed, then the stock must be shortened an amount equal to the thickness of the pad. If the stock is to be lengthened, the butt stock should be cut to a proper length to allow for the extra length of pull.

If the pitch of the original stock is satisfactory, the butt stock should be cut on a line parallel to its original surface. If the pitch is to be changed, it is necessary to cut the butt stock at the new proper angle.

A line can first be scribed, using a flexible steel rule or a transparent plastic rule. This line should be scribed with a scratch awl or a pencil at the proper angle to produce the desired pitch. Then the wood can be sawed along this line. The stock is best sawed with a finetooth "back" or "tenon" saw, but this is rather an uncommon tool and if not available, an ordinary fine-tooth hand saw can be used, taking great care, however, not to splinter the wood as the saw cuts through. After the line is scribed on the stock, transparent Scotch tape can be applied near the line, and this may help avoid some splintering.

After the butt has been cut off at the length to produce the proper length of pull and at the correct angle to secure the proper pitch, the wood must be flattened to as nearly a perfectly flat surface as possible, to insure the best possible fit between the back plate of the recoil pad and the wood. This surface can be trued up by using a piece of sandpaper on a flat file or on a flat piece of wood. When the wood is as flat as you can get it, relieve the center of the wood with a chisel so that a firm contact is insured around the outside edges when the pad is attached. Attach the pad in place now by means of screws or with screws and cement. At this point the pad will

The recoil pad has been installed. Transparent tape has been applied to the stock to protect the wood when the pad is ground down to conform to the wood.

be considerably larger than the wood. The new wood surfaces can be protected, at least to some extent, by installing Scotch tape or masking tape again around the stock next to the rubber pad.

Cutting Down the Pad and Touching Up the Stock

Rubber pads are easily ground down to size by using a sanding disk attachment on the electric drill. Care must be taken to grind the rubber to the same angle as the stock. That is, the side should be parallel to the stock and the toe and heel should be a continuation of the top and bottom line of the stock when it is finished. As the rubber is ground down, the masking tape will help to protect the original finish if care is taken in grinding.

Any small spots where the original finish has been touched by the grinding disk can be repaired by sanding them smooth with fine sandpaper and applying a mixture of white shellac and linseed oil, mixed on a one-to-one proportion. Apply this by simply moistening a small rag or cleaning patch in the mixture and rubbing it on the spots to be refinished. Several coats can be applied, if necessary, rubbing with fine sandpaper between coats. Actually this is known as the French Finish and it can be used to completely refinish the stock should you so desire. It produces a finish usually described as an oil finish.

CHAPTER 15

Towards a Better Gun Stock

TO BEGIN with a rough chunk of wood and end up with a finished gunstock is a real accomplishment for even an experienced stockmaker. I would recommend that the beginner get one of the fine, semi-inletted stock blanks and save himself much work and most of the grief of building his first gun stock. After he has had a little experience with these semi-finished projects, he will have a better understanding of the various steps that he must take in building a complete stock.

Gun Stock Blanks

Semi-inletted and machined stock blanks are available from many companies for the more common models of rifles and actions, E.C. Bishop and Reinhart Fajen, both of Warsaw, Missouri, furnish the widest variety of machined blanks. Both companies furnish different kinds of wood, such as walnut, maple, myrtlewood, laminated blanks which are made by gluing together thin sheets of walnut, or thin sheets of different kinds of woods. Laminated blanks are recommended for the greatest stability, but they are somewhat heavier since the adhesive agent is an epoxy which impregnates the thin layers of wood while bonding them together. This creates a very stable though heavier blank.

There are a number of other campanies furnishing excellent machined blanks. Among these are Roberts Wood Products, which is an especially good source for fancy grades of wood as well as of laminated blanks, and Royal Arms Company, furnisher of one of the most closely-machined blanks available—their insides being very closely-machined and the outsides being machined to almost exact size, requiring not much more than sanding. The cost of these is a little more, but they are very desirable for the inexperienced as there is less chance of ruining them through unpractised work. Unlike the Fajen and Bishop stocks, the Royal does not come with butt plate, but does have both pistol grip and forearm tip fittings.

Necessary Tools

Very few special tools are needed to fit and finish the semi-inletted stock blanks. Guidescrews, which are simply rods threaded at one end to fit into the guardscrew holes of the bolt-action, can be obtained at a low price from various gunsmith suppliers. A pair can be used with actions having parallel guardscrews, while only one guidescrew is needed with an action wherein the rear screw enters the receiver at an angle. These guidescrews are used to let the receiver down through the guardscrew holes already provided in most inletted stock blanks.

The minimum tools required for stockmaking are: at least one round chisel about ¾ in.; three flat chisels, ¼ in., ⅜ in. and ½ in.; a small inexpensive set of carving tools, which can be found at a low price. These contain small gouges and chisels (commonly called carving tools) capable of getting into small areas. You will also need some checkering tools. A very fine set is supplied by Frank Mittermeier consisting of three tools, directions, a set of templates and a set of patterns, all costing about two or three dollars. This inexpensive set is adequate for the amateur and makes him capable of doing a very fine job.

Inletting the Action

For ease of explanation, we will fit a bolt-action rifle with a new inletted stock blank. First strip the receiver of all parts, then install the guidescrews.

Paint the lower surfaces of the barrel and action with some kind of coloring agent. The one most commonly used is a mixture of lampblack and oil. This is available at most paint stores, but you can mix your own from heavy oil and lampblack which can be secured at the drug store. The mixture is painted over the lower surface of the barrel and action, so that when it is let into the semi-inletted blank, being guided by the pins or guidescrews, the black will adhere to the wood at the points of contact. Then where these points touch, wood can be removed with a chisel. Proceed with caution so as to get as near a perfect fit as possible. The first requirement for making a fine stock is a great deal of time and patience. The barrel and action should be inletted into the wood to half the diameter of the barrel and receiver—that is when finished, the wood should come just half-way up the sides of the barrel.

As the work proceeds, great care must be taken to keep the barrel and action from "rocking." The back side of the recoil lug on a bolt-action must be fitted very tightly against the wood, especially the area just back of the recoil lug, and the bottom of the rear tang must make firm contact in the wood, so that when the guardscrews are tightened, the re-

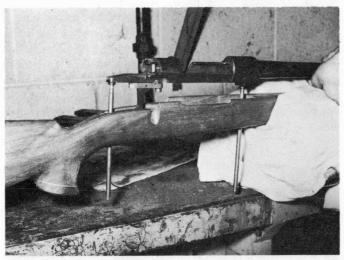

Showing the use of the guidescrews when inletting a Mauser barrel and receiver into a semi-inletted stock blank.

ceiver tang will not be sprung downward as this in turn would raise the barrel out of the stock. A good way to check the bedding of a bolt-action, when the job is finished, is to slowly loosen the rear guardscrew, carefully observing whether the tang of the action moves upward. The same thing can be repeated with the front screw. Any strain placed on the receiver when the guardscrew is tightened is detrimental to accuracy. This is especially true of the Mauser 98, which has a long, slim rear tang. The long, slim tang makes for a graceful pistol grip, but at the same time it is easily sprung. This is the reason a ferrule is always supplied with a Mauser. This fits around the rear guardscrew and acts as a spacer between the triggerguard and the receiver. It is a common practice among American stockmakers to discard this ferrule, but it is one of the essential parts of the Mauser action and should always be installed in the stock. Since the ferrule is furnished in exactly the right length, it holds the triggerguard and receiver in

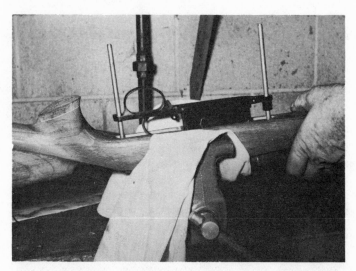

After the barrel and receiver have been inletted into the stock, the guide-screws can be used to lead the trigger guard into the proper position.

proper relationship to each other. It also prevents springing the receiver.

RELIEVING STRESS   After the barreled-action has been completely inletted, the wood at the very end of the rear tang must be relieved. A space of 1/32 in. is about right. This prevents the wood from cracking when the rifle is fired. Recoil will invariably "set" the metal parts back slightly and if the wood fits too tightly around the rear tang, it will crack or split out. Sometimes a tight fit at this point will split the grip if recoil is heavy; sometimes a "chip" will come loose. A 1/32 in. space prevents these troubles.

Forming and Finishing the New Stock

FINAL SHAPING   After the stock has been finish-inletted, the butt cut off at the proper length of pull and the recoil pad or butt plate installed, the wood is then dressed down so as to fit evenly with the metal parts. This is best done before any bluing is done, since it is very difficult to prevent scratching the metal while the wood is worked, even if you are extremely careful.

Some semi-inletted stock blanks need no final shaping. An example of this are the blanks furnished by the Royal Arms Company. Some semi-machined stock blanks require considerable work on the outside to bring them down to proper size and shape. If so; this is done by the use of various woodworking tools, mainly wood rasps, files, and so forth.

It is usually best for the beginner to start with a semi-machined blank which needs nothing but final sanding. The initial cost of such a blank is a little higher, but well worth it, since it nullifies to a great extent the chance that an inexperienced workman will make some of the otherwise very common mistakes in shaping the stock. The blanks furnished by the Royal Arms Co. and some similar companies require only sanding after they have been inletted. After a workman has made one or more of these, he has a little better idea of what he is trying to do and can then undertake a blank that will require more knowledge, imagination and work. Fajen now supplies a universal pattern stock blank which can be worked down to almost any style.

SANDING   After inletting and fitting the metal parts, start with the #180-grit production sandpaper, and sand the stock as smooth as possible. The #180 production sandpaper is sometimes described as open-coat sandpaper, and it is superior to ordinary sandpaper because it does not have a tendency to clog or fill up.

The wood must then be "whiskered." This is done by wetting the wood—by applying water to it with a wet cloth. This will raise the grain and cause the wood surfaces to become very rough. This roughness is very easily removed by again using the #180-grit sandpaper after the wood has dried. Low heat may be applied to speed the drying.

Next, sand with a finer-grade sandpaper. A good one is #240 grit. Sometimes sandpaper is designated by numbers, as #1, #1½, #2, #2-0, #3-0, etc. Using #240 grit or its equivalent, again sand the stock as smooth as possible, always being very careful to maintain square edges and sharp corners where they should be left sharp, for example, along the top of the forearm, the edge of the cheekpiece, the pistol-grip cap, etc.

After sanding with the #240 grit, the wood should again be whiskered by wetting, allowed to dry, and then resanding. Resand now using #320-grit paper or its equivalent. Whiskering and sanding with fine sandpaper should be repeated until the grain will no longer raise through wetting.

FINISHING   When the sanding job is finished, any porous wood must be filled. Commercial fillers may be secured from a gunsmith supplier or from a paint store. Any of these will work all right if used according to directions. One commonly used by stock makers is white shellac mixed half-and-half with alcohol. This can be applied to the wood with a brush, allowed to dry, and then sanded off down to the wood. Sometimes several coats are needed. This is one of the best ways to fill a gun stock because it does not fill its pores with anything to discolor it.

The final finish may consist of oil, varnish, lacquer, plastic or other material. The best of all gun finishes is oil, and when we speak of an oil finish on a gunstock, we always refer to linseed oil in some form. Special preparations are now on the market which speed up the finishing process. They produce a satisfactory oil finish in a minimum of time if the simple directions on the bottle or can are followed.

Some of the advantages of an oil finish are durability, lack of gaudiness, it never comes off in patches, and it can be maintained easily and quickly by rubbing on another coat of oil.

There are plastic finishes which work well. One type comes in a spray can. It produces a fairly durable finish with a high gloss characteristic which appeals to some people. These also must be applied strictly according to directions. One of these preparations is supplied by the Schuetzen Gun Works, 1226 Prairie Road, Colorado Springs, Colorado. This one comes in an aerosol can, which facilitates the application. It results in a shiny, durable finish, easy to apply. There are other plastic finishes, furnished by gunsmith supply houses which consist of two ingredients, namely resin and a hardener. This kind of plastic finish is a little harder to apply, but it results in a good durable finish when properly applied.

Lacquer is another finish widely used. Many factory stocks are finished in lacquer. This can also be procured in aerosol cans.

Varnish is no longer extensively used because of its tendency to scratch and chip. Some of the old-timers used the highest-grade spar varnish in connection with linseed oil. They applied it with a soft pad on which a drop or two of linseed oil and a few drops of spar varnish had been applied, and then rubbed the stock vigorously with a circular motion until the surface had been thoroughly covered.

The French Finish is a mixture of white shellac and oil— half-and-half proportion. This is also applied as just described. In both of these finishes, the material must be applied sparingly, over and over until after several coats the finish is built to desired thickness and quality. But as to the last two finishes, while these result in durable and beautiful finishes, they are tricky and are not recommended to the inexperienced workmen.

Check the list of suppliers for additional sources of materials.

Installing Sling Swivels

The quick-detachable type of sling swivel for rifles is more popular but also more expensive than the non-detachable type. There are several methods of attaching sling-swivel bases to the stock, but the one most commonly used is just simply to screw them into the wood.

The rear base is simply a form of eyebolt with a wood-screw thread which can be screwed into the butt stock. The front base is about the same except that it consists of an eyebolt with a machine screw for which the nut is serrated or grooved on the outside. Sling swivels are placed at varying distances apart, usually averaging from 26 in. to 28 in., with the rear base installed about 3 in. forward of the toe of the stock. This can vary from 2 in. to 4 in., depending on the length of the stock, and the distance between the two swivels varies also with the length of the butt stock and the length of the forearm. For stocks of standard dimensions, the distance of 3 in. from the toe is about right, with a spacing of approximately 27 in. between front and rear swivels.

An instruction paper will usually accompany the new set of swivels, but remember that in many instances you will have to actually drill two holes for each swivel. Usually you can quickly identify the swivel that goes up front on the forearm by its special retaining nut which, when installed, will press firmly into the wood and not protrude against the barrel. While this assembly takes care of holding the forward swivel base in place, the rear swivel, by contrast, will be held by its screw going right into the wood. For this to be a secure fastening, its screw hole must be just the right size—not too big, however, the upper part of the hole toward the stock surface generally has to be drilled out larger to accommodate the cylindrical or tubular-shaped portion of the screw base so that the swivel, when mounted, will not only swivel, attach and detach efficiently, but also not protrude unduly from the stock.

To install the lower or rear quick-detachable type swivel, mark its location with a small prick punch. For making the first hole, which will be made only about ¼ in. deep, select a drill correctly matching the size of the major diameter of the screw. With either an electric drill or a hand drill, drill this hole at the location marked. Use reasonable care in making this hole so that it will be at right angles to the surface of the stock or, in other words, so that its walls, when you're through, will be surrounded by the best balanced thickness of stock wood. Generally this doesn't offer much of a problem although the stock surfaces, where this swivel is installed, tend to narrow to a rather sharply-rounded configuration giving plenty of strength fore and aft, but far less to each side. Hold the depth of this hole to only that necessary to indent that part of the swivel base that you don't want protruding from the wood.

Next use a smaller drill, one which is about the size of the minor diameter of the screw, to drill the hole deeper, preferably to a depth slightly greater than the depth of the screw. This smaller hole will be the one actually gripping the screw and holding the swivel base to the stock. The swivel base can then be screwed into the wood, using a small punch through its eye hole for turning leverage, if necessary. If the base is quick-detachable, it is not screwed quite all the way in; as you turn it in, watch the fit of the large-diameter portion of the screw in the first hole you made, since correct fit will prevent the wood from splitting.

The hole for the front base is located in the same general manner. Care should be taken to make sure that it is centered and straight—that is, vertical to the forearm.

On the forearm some prefer to drill the hole from the inside. But this is not a good idea because as the drill comes through the wood, the wood is apt to splinter, making an unsightly surface around the swivel base. The best way is to drill the hole from the outside or the bottom of the forearm.

This one is drilled all the way through into the barrel channel. This hole must then be slightly counterdrilled to a larger size so as to accept the retaining nut which will be pressed into the wood on the side nearest the barrel. The body of this nut is smooth so select a drill of the same size as the smooth portion of this nut. The top of the nut is corrugated and somewhat larger than the body, so that when the nut is pressed into the wood, the corrugations will prevent the nut from turning when the swivel base is screwed into it. The retaining nut must be fitted below the surface of the wood in the barrel channel so that it will not interfere with the barrel when the latter is replaced in the stock. Sometimes this screw must be shortened a little to prevent such interference.

The installation of the plain non-detachable swivels is done in the same manner.

CHAPTER 16

Converting
Military Guns to
Sporting Rifles

AFTER EACH of the World Wars, our returning soldiers brought back many foreign Service rifles, either as souvenirs or as the makings for a custom-built sporting rifle. Many others have bought U.S. surplus military rifles or rifles from those selling the surplus of other governments. Most military rifles are safe enough for any cartridge for which they were made. It is ridiculous to think that any government is equipping its armies with booby-traps that will explode and kill its own men. But many military guns are clumsy, and by the time you have converted them to sporting rifles, the cost may be beyond that of a good sporting rifle made from such actions as the FN, etc. However, many will make fine sporting rifles. There is general agreement that the Model 98 Mauser, for instance, makes an extremely fine sporting rifle, and this model is usually given first place. The 1903 Service Rifle (known as the Springfield) and the 1917 Service Rifle (known as the Enfield) place second and third either in this order or vice versa.

Notes on Suitable Actions

MAUSER ACTIONS   There are many varieties of the Mauser actions. All are good, but some are better than others. The most desirable of these is the Model 98 and its modifications, which are very similar to it. Among these are the Model 1909 Argentine, the Peruvian, the Costa Rican, the Mexican, the Kar 98, the Gew 98, and others. The Model 1924 is often known as the Yugoslavian action, and "1924" is usually stamped on its receiver ring. The main difference between the Model 1924 and the Model 98 is length, the 1924 being considerably shorter than the 98. Model 98 receivers manufactured during World War I were somewhat softer than receivers manufactured after 1924, and for hot cartridges some of the older Model 98 receivers should be re-heat treated.

Some of the Mauser-type rifles such as the Spanish M93, the Swedish M94, the Brazilian M94, the Chilean M95, the Uruguayan, Peruvian, Chinese, Transvaal, Orange Free State, and Serbian M99 are all suitable for conversion to certain modern cartridges. In actual blow-up tests, these older M93 and M95 actions have withstood loads almost as heavy as other common bolt-actions, but it is generally considered that the safety factor on these rifles is not as good as with the M98 and its modifications, which have the extra or safety-lug.

Some of the European Mausers sporterized in Europe have deep dovetails cut across the top of the receiver ring for the installation of telescope bases. Judging by blow-up tests, this weakens the action. Anyone wishing to buy a European Mauser with typical European mount bases, should avoid buying a gun having this deep dovetail in the receiver ring. Also, many European rifles sold in this country after World War I were quite elaborately engraved. In many instances the actions were annealed before the engraving was done, and were not re-heat treated afterwards. This left the receiver very soft, which allowed the action to develop dangerous headspace.

SPRINGFIELDS These days everyone hears and reads about high- and low-number Springfields. Prior to World War II, the 1903 Springfield rifle was manufactured in two government arsenals, one located at Springfield, Massachusetts, and one at Rock Island, Illinois. The early 1903 Springfields were made of what is now described as poor material, merely carbon steel, casehardened. This casehardening was done relatively deeply, which rendered thin sections of the receiver glass-hard all the way through. Sometimes these old receivers will shatter if dropped on the floor. During World War II at the government arsenal at Ogden, Utah, thousands of these old actions were fitted with modern Springfield bolts. Elmer Keith test-fired each of these rifles with five bluepill, .30-06 loads and none showed any weakness. These old actions should never be fitted with any other make bolts.

The 1903 receiver manufactured at Springfield was this old hardened type with serial numbers under 800,000 and at Rock Island with numbers under 285,507. A Springfield in the 800,-000 to 1,275,967 series was double heat-treated, which consisted of the old casehardening plus a drawing or tempering process which rendered the receiver much tougher than the older method. In 1928, beginning with #1,275,767, the receivers manufactured at the Springfield Arsenal were made of nickel steel, and at the Rock Island Arsenal, the nickel steel was used after #285,509.

Just before World War II, Remington Arms Company took up the manufacture of the 1903 rifle. Also the Smith-Corona Company, under government contract, made the 1903 A3 and A4. Most of these World War II actions were made of alloy steel known as "National Emergency Steel." They were apparently well heat-treated and were strong. However, their workmanship in no way compared with that of those from Rock Island and Springfield Arsenals.

After World War I, the bolt-actions became increasingly popular and some gunsmiths were especially active in "sporterizing" Springfields. The Sedgley Co. started sporterizing these rifles on a production basis. The sporterizing usually consisted of the installation of a high-priced stock and high-priced sights plus a blue job. Ads said that the rifles had been re-heat-treated, but the heat-treating consisted merely of annealing the receiver to a dangerous degree. A soft receiver, however, will stand tremendous proof-loads without injury to the shooter. Actually, they were more dangerous than the casehardened receiver in its original condition. These "heat-treated" receivers, like many which had been through a fire, would rapidly develop headspace to a dangerous degree and ultimately many of them blew up.

There were other hybrid actions sold between the two World Wars, by certain dealers in surplus arms and materials. Some of these consisted of low-number Springfield receivers with altered M17 (Enfield) bolts. Most of these hybrids were dangerous, especially with modern ammunition.

THE KRAGS   Much has been said about the 1903 and 1917 Service rifles. The predecessor to the 1903 was the Krag Jorgensen, caliber .30-40, known as the Krag, or more affectionately, "the old Krag." The Krag was probably the smoothest bolt-action ever produced. The Norwegian Krag was somewhat stronger. The American Krag was manufactured between 1894 and 1903. It had only one locking lug at the fore-end of the bolt and a rather long and big safety lug on the side of the bolt. The bolt-handle also acted as a safety lug. Generally speaking, the Krag is suitable only for the .30-40. The magazine consists of a big box on the side of the receiver which opens out. This is disliked by some, but it was the most easily-loaded magazine ever produced. A shooter with cold hands could merely dump a handful of cartridges in the box, slam it shut and proceed to shoot. The Krag was sold to the

public through the Division of Civilian Marksmanship for
$2.50 each. Currently a Krag in perfect condition is probably
fifty times that much. The .30-40 is still a highly-desirable
cartridge and the Krag is still a highly-desirable rifle.

MANNLICHER ACTIONS   Since World War II, large numbers
of Mannlicher actions have been sold through special outlets.
Most Mannlichers exhibit the highest degree of workmanship
and they are considered one of the smoothest operating actions there is. They have a rotary-type magazine, and while
it is one of the smoothest in existence, it is invariably made
for one cartridge and will handle no other; at least, it will
handle no other without a tremendous amount of alteration
work which is usually impossible for even an accomplished
gunsmith. In practical terms, this means that any Mannlicher
should not be altered to any other cartridge than the one for
which it was designed. For example, a large number of Greek
Mannlichers have been sold to the American shooting public.
These were designed for the 6.5x54 Mannlicher cartridge
which is currently manufactured by Norma and is available
at most large sporting goods stores. Since this is an excellent
cartridge in its own right, the Greek Mannlicher should be
rebarreled only for its original 6.5x54 cartridge.

The Mannlicher is not well adapted for the use of a telescope sight, mainly because of its split-bridge design, so they
are best used with some type of iron sight. They can be altered
for scope use and there are several telescope mounts available
that can be put on them, but all of these involve considerable
expense and the work involved is beyond the ability of the
amateur gun enthusiast.

There are still other military rifles which are of interest
to collectors and hunters who desire to avoid extensive sporterizing projects. In this class of rifle we have two Japanese
military models; the SMLE-type British Enfield, the caliber
.303; some Russian models; the Italian Carcano; and various
other modified or hybrid models.

JAPANESE ACTIONS   Two Japanese rifles are extremely strong, the 6.5mm being the strongest military of those tested by the author. Tests have also shown the 7.7mm Japanese action to be relatively strong. Both offer the highest degree of gas protection and a relatively good breeching system. But they are quite undesirable from the standpoint of sporting use. They are rough in operation; they cannot be converted from any practical standpoint; the safety is practically useless for sporting purposes; and from the standpoint of desirability (which should not be confused with strength), they are not worth spending much time and money on. Sure, the bolt can be converted for a low scope, and a Timney Trigger with side-safety can be installed. If you intend to use the gun, this should be installed anyway because the original trigger is atrocious. Ammunition for the Japanese calibers is now available from most dealers handling Norma products. The 6.5mm may be worth an inexpensive restocking job. The 6.5mm is a relatively short action and adaptable only for short cartridges.

There is one Japanese action which is *unsafe* and should not be used. This is the one which is simply made of cast iron. The two safe actions that were earlier mentioned have removable upper tangs, while the cast iron model has a large tang, case in one piece with its receiver. When this action is removed from its stock, it has all the sorry appearance of cast iron, and this model should *never* be considered for conversion or use.

Readily Available Accessories

TYPICAL TRIGGER AND SAFETY KITS   The various military models have some undesirable characteristics from a sporting standpoint and many of these undesirable features are common to all. For example, the trigger pull on most military Mausers is quite unsatisfactory for sporting use and most of these actions are not suitable for the installation of telescope sights without considerable alteration. The exceptions to this are the P14 and the 1917 Enfield, on which the bolt-handle and safety are ideal for scope use without any alteration. The 1903 Service Rifle and the Model 98 Mauser require the bolt-handle to be altered to clear a low-mounted scope, and the original safety, since it interferes with the scope, must be replaced by a new one of some kind. New ones often incorporate the trigger mechanism.

There is available from Timney (see list of suppliers) a trigger mechanism with a built-in side-safety. Adjustments are provided in this trigger which allow a very satisfactory single-stage trigger. Jaeger and Dayton-Traister also have safeties available for installation.

TYPICAL UP-COCK KITS　　The two Enfields have what is considered by most as an undesirable feature—a forward cocking action. All this means is that the cocking action takes place as the bolt moves forward into its lock position, as compared with the "cock-on-opening" feature of the M98 Mauser. The advantage of the cock-on-opening action is that most of the compression of the mainspring takes place as the bolt-handle is raised up. With this system you can handle the cocking compression much easier with one hand while *raising* the bolt-handle than is the case if you have to exert a hard push to cock the gun while pushing the handle forward since this, in fact, tends to push the entire gun away from you. But the Enfield bolt can easily be converted to "cock-on-opening" by the installation of special kits supplied by two or three manufacturers. These kits consist of the adjustable trigger described above, a special cocking piece and a special speedlock and mainspring. These special speedlock, up-cock trigger kits are easily installed by anyone who has a hand grinder, or they may even be installed by anyone having a file, if enough perseverance is used.

Two manufacturers of these special speedlock, up-cock trigger kits are Viggo Miller and the Dayton-Traister Company. The Viggo Miller kit is very simple and very satisfactory. This kit is relatively inexpensive and consists of a special cocking piece and a small detachable-cam which is inserted in the rear end of the bolt. These parts are very easily installed without the aid of special tools. This kit utilizes the original trigger. Viggo Miller also furnishes a trigger-adjusting attachment which eliminates the preliminary stage or the slack, in the original trigger mechanism. This also can be installed without the aid of special tools.

The early Mausers, 1889 to 1896, did not have the "cock-on-opening" feature, but instead cocked as the bolt was pushed forward. They should not be tampered with and are best left as they originally were. About the only alteration necessary or desirable for these old Mausers is to install a good trigger, a low-line safety, and alter the bolt-handle so it will take a low scope. The first of these alterations the gun owner can take care of for himself, by the purchase of one of the kits mentioned. It would be best to take the job of altering the bolt to a good gunsmith, as the bolt may too easily be ruined while being heated.

TRIGGERGUARDS   Many gun enthusiasts consider the military Mauser triggerguard rather bulky and unattractive. The triggerguard of most bolt-actions consists of the magazine box and triggerguard all machined in one piece and usually referred to as "milled guards." Some Mausers and Springfields made toward the end of World War II were equipped with "stamped guards." It is desirable to replace these with the milled type. The Mauser milled guard, or more specifically the guard bow, can be slimmed or streamlined by the judicious use of a file and grinder. This streamlining should not be carried to an extreme as is sometimes seen, but the bow can be narrowed some at the rear, then polished to give a more pleasing appearance. The Springfield milled guard in its original form is quite attractive enough and needs no alteration.

Enfield Improvements

REMOVING ENFIELD EARS   When making the Enfield into a Sporter, something must be done with the Enfield "ears." The original Enfield has a rear sight mounted on top of the receiver

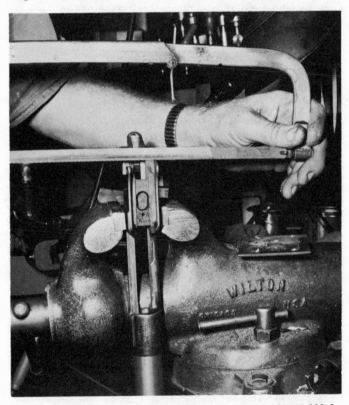

Removing Enfield ears with a hacksaw. Use the best tungsten hi-speed blade. One of the several blades on the market carries the Remington name.

bridge (rear end of the receiver) which is protected by a shield on each side. These shields are generally referred to as the "Enfield Ears."

In order to make the Enfield into an attractive sporter, these ears must be removed. The amateur gunsmith can remove these ears by sawing, filing or grinding them off. A hacksaw fitted with a tungsten high-speed blade will easily saw off these ears, *if only mild pressure* is used on the saw. If too much pressure is used on the saw, or if you try to remove the ears too fast, the steel will harden and ruin the hacksaw blade.

If the saw has been pushed too hard and caused the ears to harden, or if an Enfield is found that is too hard to saw, it will be necessary to soften the side of the ears at the point where they are to be cut. Slowly heat the ears, mainly in the areas to be cut, to a black color. Watch the colors carefully as the heating proceeds, first yellow, then brown, then blue, and finally black. This will all occur before red heat is reached. When the color turns black, allow the action to cool. Then it should be soft enough to saw easily.

Once the ears have been removed by sawing or grinding, the bridge can be dressed down with a file to conform almost exactly with the contour of the receiver ring (the front end of the receiver). When filing the receiver bridge to the same contour as the receiver ring, a straightedge placed on the receiver ring so that it will just barely clear the bridge will be helpful, thus enabling you to shape the bridge to exactly the height and contour of the ring. A close match is quite important. Especially when it comes to installing new sights.

SCOPE MOUNTS FOR THE ENFIELD   The old M30 Remington bolt-action rifle was merely a modified 1917 Enfield with its ears removed and contoured to conform to the receiver ring. This means that the altered military Enfield will accept any scope mount designed for the M30 Remington. There are also special Enfield scope mounts available.

Glossary

Action: The action of a rifle is the actual firing mechanism or the complete mechanism of the firearm exclusive of the barrel and stock.

Anneal: To anneal steel or other metals is to render it soft, and it is usually accomplished by heating it to a red color and allowing it to cool gradually.

Barrel: A steel tube of a firearm through which the projectile is driven and the part which directs the projectile toward its target.

Bore: The interior or the hole through the barrel. Rifle and pistol bores are usually measured in fractions of an inch and in millemeters. Rifle bores contain the rifling made up of lands and grooves.

Breech Bolt: The part of the action which closes the breech or the part whch locks the cartridge in place. The word "bolt" is commonly applied to this part in bolt-action rifles and semi-automatic rifles, but in some instances such as falling-block, single-shot actions, the corresponding part is called a breech-block. In repeating rifles of the lever-action type, such as the Winchester and Marlin, this part could be called either bolt or breechblock.

Bullet: The projectile for a firearm. Projectiles are made in many shapes, sizes and of many different materials. The most common type of bullet is the regular, solid, cast bullet made from lead or some alloy of lead. A regular jacketed bullet consists of a jacket made of copper or an alloy of copper or steel with a lead core. Jacketed bullets are made in several types such as hollow-point, soft-point, or full metal-patched. Soft and hollow-pointed bullets are sometimes called dum-dums. The term "dum-dum" applies more or less to bullets that will upset or expand upon impact. Some jacketed bullets are made with bronze or steel points and special types of bullets are made which are called armor-piercing, incendiary, etc.

Butt: That part of the gun stock whch comes in contact with the shoulder of the shooter.

Butt Plate: Plate used to cover the end or butt of the stock. It is made from various types of material such as metal, horn, plastic or rubber.

Caliber: The actual diameter of the bore of a rifle. It is commonly measured in two ways: 1. By the actual bore diameter, 2. By the groove diameter.

Cam: In guns—usually takes the form of a slanting surface which, when rotated, will move a contacted part backward or forward. Cams are commonly used in firearm actions to accomplish the actual locking operation or to accomplish other functions such as cocking.

Cannelure: A depression or groove rolled into a bullet or cartridge case. The cannelure in a bullet can be plain or knurled and it sometimes functions to crimp the cartridge down to retain the bullet in place. Another function is to help hold the lead core within the jacket. A cannelure on a case is simply a groove rolled in the neck at the proper point to keep the bullet from sliding too far into the case. Lead bullets have numerous cannelures for the retention of grease or lubricant.

Cap: A metal covering for a pistol grip or the end of a forearm. It is also used in connection with percussion caps used for detonating muzzle-loading firearms of the percussion-cap type. Such caps are usually referred to as caps instead of percussion caps.

Carburizing: (carbonizing) Heat treatment of low carbon steel to introduce carbon into the surface which produces a hard skin when quenched.

Carbine: A short rifle commonly used by troops on horseback. Still in military use in varied applications.

Cartridge: The fixed ammunition of metallic type for a firearm. A cartridge is an assembly of (1) case, (2) primer, (3) powder charge, (4) bullet or projectile. Therefore, the word cartridge applies to the four component parts assembled into one element.

Cast-off: The distance a stock is offset to the right from the line of sight or from the axis of the bore.

Cast-on: The term used when the stock offset is to the left. Cast-off is commonly used for the right-handed shooter; cast-on for the left-handed one.

Center-fire: This term applies to a firearm which uses a cartridge with the primer in its center; or to a cartridge with a primer in its center.

Center Punch: A punch with a short sharp point for making marks on metal. The term "center-punch" is used synonymously with the term "prick-punch."

Chamber: The enlarged recess in the breech of a firearm which is provided to accept the cartridge or shell.

Chasers: Special tools for cutting threads.

Checkering: Applies to diamond-shaped patterns cut in wood or metal parts for the purposes of minimizing slippage, and for the purpose of ornamentation.

Cheekpiece: A projection or raised portion of a gun stock which affords a better rest or more surface for the cheek of the shooter at the time of firing a rifle or shotgun.

Choke: Refers to the constriction in the muzzle of shotgun barrels. Choke is put into shotgun barrels to improve· the pattern.

Cocking piece: A piece attached to the projecting end of the firing-pin in bolt-action rifles. Cocking pieces are normally made in two styles, head and headless. A good example of the head-type is the 1903 Springfield, which has a large head or knob on the large end of the cocking piece which can be grasped with the thumb and forefinger, thus enabling the shooter to manually cock his rifle. The headless type of cocking piece is either plain or has a small groove or some provision for the insertion of a cartridge rim or screwdriver or some other tool to allow withdrawal of the cocking piece and thus cock the firearm in case of misfire, without the necessity of unlocking the bolt with the accompanying danger of the misfire being due to a hangfire or delayed-action, which could cause the firearm to blow up.

Comb: The top of the butt stock or the part of the stock which extends from the heel to a point just back of the hand as the stock is grasped. It is the part of the stock on which the cheek rests at the time of firing.

Cordite: A type of powder used by the English to designate smokeless. A nitroglycerine base powder, actually a form of dynamite and one extremely hard on the bore of a rifle. It is still a popular propellant in England, especially for big-bore rifles used in Africa.

Crossbolt: A transverse bolt used to lock the standing breech and barrels of a shotgun together.

Crosshair: A type of reticule consisting of fine crossed wires or hairs to designate the center of the optical field in a telescope sight.

Cut Off: A part found in some rifle actions which can be arranged to temporarily prevent cartridges from feeding from the magazine into the chamber when the bolt or mechanism is operated.

Cylinder: Usually applied to the part of the revolver which contains the cartridge chambers and which revolves so that each cartridge lines up in turn with the barrel. It is used also in connection with the description of a rifle barrel and applies to that part of the barrel which extends just forward of the receiver.

Damascus: A type of ornamental metal used in the manufacture of shotgun barrels. Damascus applies to a combination of metals or different types of the same metal produced by welding or twisting together dissimilar strips. Barrels made from Damascus steels are completely obsolete in the United States today because of their lack of tensile strength or inability to hold the pressures of modern shells; however, it is still available in some makes of European shot guns.

Dies: A term which can apply to numerous or several items in reference to guns, the most important of which are thread-cutting dies; cartridge-reloading and sizing dies; and dies for the production of various types of parts commonly called stamps, which are found so often in modern firearms.

Drop: The distance from the line of sight to the top of the heel or point of comb of the stock or forearm. Often drop is specified from the line of sight and also from the axis to the bore, since the gunmaker is often called upon to build a rifle complete with stocks, but without sights.

Ejector: A device to expel the fired cartridge case from the action of the rifle after it has been fired. Ejectors are commonly of two types, plain and automatic.

Escutcheon: A reinforcement border or bushing through which a screw or screws, or other fastening device, passes.

Express: A term usually applied to denote a rifle or cartridge of higher than usual velocities.

Extractor: The part, usually shaped in the form of a hook and attached to the bolt or breechblock or other part of a rifle or shotgun, which withdraws the fired cartridge case from the chamber of a firearm. It is the part which actually extracts or withdraws the fired case from the chamber, the case later being expelled by the ejector.

Flute: A groove in various types of tools such as reamers, drills and taps.

Flux: A substance or mixture of substances or chemicals used to facilitate the bonding of metals together by means of soluble brazing or welding. Fluxes are commonly made in the form of powder, pastes and liquids.

Forearm: The portion of the stock which is forward of the receiver and directly under the barrel of a firearm. It is sometimes called the fore-end, especially with respect to shotguns wherein the wooden stock is made up of two pieces. While it is a separate piece in the case of a two-piece stock, it is simply the forward part of a one-piece stock such as in the rifle commonly described as a Sporter.

Forging: One method of working or shaping metals.

Gauge (gage): A term used for the designation of shotgun bore sizes. Standard shotgun bores, ranging from the smallest to the largest, are: 28, 20, 16, 12 and 10. Old guns were often made in 8-gauge, but 8-gauge guns are now illegal in the United States. .410 is usually referred to as a gauge, but this is really a caliber, being the actual measurement of the bore.

Grip: The small part of the stock which is grasped by the hand. It is also used to designate the handle of a pistol or revolver.

Guard: The term applies to the loop, usually made of metal, plastic or horn, curving around the trigger to protect it. It is commonly called the triggerguard in some types of firearms.

Hammer: The part of a gun or rifle action that strikes the firing-pin to fire the cartridge within the chamber. Guns are sometimes referred to as hammerless, but all guns have some type of hammer or corresponding parts such as the cocking piece. The word "hammer" as applied to hammer guns refers to outside hammers which can be cocked by hand. In some hammer guns the hammer is cocked when the lever or slide is operated. Others must be cocked manually every time the firearm is fired. The word hammerless applies to a gun where the hammers are enclosed or concealed inside the action.

Hand: The lever or dog which turns the cylinder of a revolver. The hand is attached to the trigger or hammer and when the hammer is pulled back to cocked position, the hand is actuated and turns the cylinder into position for the next shot.

Hang–fire: A term used to describe a delayed action or delayed ignition when the trigger is pulled, the firing mechanism strikes the primer of a cartridge, but nothing happens until an instant later. It can result in a disaster or a blown-up gun if the shooter does not wait long enough to determine whether it is actually a misfire or a hang-fire. In the event it is a hang-fire and the bolt or locking mechanism is opened too soon, the cartridge will explode when it is moved partly or completely out of the chamber but still in the action of the gun.

Hinge Pin: The pin upon which the barrel or barrels of shotguns hinge.

Improved cartridge: A form of a wildcat cartridge usually made by fire-forming the cartridge. A factory cartridge can be fired in a slightly altered chamber, thus blowing the case out to create a wildcat or improved cartridge. This means a rifle chambered for one of these cartridges will still handle factory ammunition.

Knurling: The checking of metal to produce a rough surface.

Lands: A term used to describe the space between the grooves of a rifle barrel. It also describes the space or ridges between the flutes on reamers and other tools which have flutes.

Lap: A piece of soft metal in the form of a plug or other shape which can be charged with abrasive and used for fine grinding or polishing. Lapping barrels is a common job which a gunsmith is requred to do.

Mainspring: The spring which operates the firing-pin or hammer; usually it is this spring's force which detonates the primer.

Magazine: The part of a repeating firearm which receives the cartridges, from which they are fed into the chamber when the repeating mechanism is operated. There are numerous types of magazines such as box, tubular, rotary, etc.

Magnum: In connection with firearms it serves to designate rifles using extremely large, powerful cartridges. It is also used to describe a firearm of greater-than-average power.

Monte Carlo: A form of stock in which the comb extends horizontally or parallel to the axis of the bore to within a short distance of the heel, where it descends abruptly to the heel portion. On rifles, a Monte Carlo stock is popular with target shooters for it helps them use target-type sights which are mounted necessarily rather high above the bore. It is also quite popular among shotgun trapshooters.

Nipple: The tube which receives the percussion cap of a muzzle-loading or percussion-loading firearm. It is a small projection through which there is an opening leading to the powder charge in the barrel. Upon detonation, the flash from the cap is carried through the opening in the nipple, into the powder charge in the barrel.

Paradox: A shotgun in which the forward portion of the barrel is rifled. It was thought that the rifling in the last few inches of the bore would allow the use of solid balls to a better advantage and at the same time retain the advantage of handling a charge of shot fairly well. Such guns are not popular or common in the United States, but they have been used extensively in South Africa.

Pistol Grip: The part of the gun stock which turns down just to the rear of the trigger, forming a handle similar to that used on a pistol or revolver. Stocks are made either with a pistol grip or a plain grip.

Pitch: A term used to describe the angle of the butt of the firearm in relation to the bore or line of sight. It is also used to describe the distance from the center of one screw thread or gear tooth to the center of the next. If a screw has ten threads to the inch, it is said to have a pitch of ten.

Ramp: An incline. A front sight of a large type which is a long slanting piece of metal, attached to the muzzle-end of a barrel and provided with a means for holding the front sight. Actually, it is a base for the front sight.

Reamer: A tool used to enlarge an already existing hole. For example, a hole is drilled and then reamed to exact size.

Revolver: A type of repeating firearm which has a revolving cylinder containing chambers for the cartridges.

Sear: That part of a firing mechanism which engages the hammer or cocking piece. It holds the hammer in cocked position until the trigger is pulled. The sear is usually an integral part of the trigger, but sometimes it is separate.

Set-Trigger: A trigger mechanism designed for lightening the trigger pull. There are many types of set-trigger mechanism, both double and single. With a double-set style, one trigger is pulled or pushed to "set", the other trigger can then be released by the slightest touch. With single-set trigger mechanisms, the normal procedure is to move the trigger itself ahead until it catches in the forward position, at which time only the slightest pressure is required to set it off. Set-triggers of various types are popular among target shooters, but they are not used very extensively for hunting purposes.

Schnabel: The tip of the forearm, usually taking some form such as a knob or enlarged section.

Tang: The extension of an action used to attach the metal parts to the wood. Some types of actions have long tangs extending well down both top and bottom of the grip. Tang sights are sights which are designed to attach to the upper tang of a rifle.

Toe: The lower rear extremity of the butt stock, or its point which comes nearest the arm pit.

Wildcat: A cartridge for which no factory ammunition is available.

List of Suppliers

Allenite Mfg. Co., 1809 N. Milwaukee, Chicago, Ill. 60647	Electric grinder with attachments
Alley Supply Co., Box 458, Sonora, Calif. 95370	General supplies
Anderson Gunshop, 1203 Broadway, Yakima, Wash. 98902	Plastic stock finish, bedding kits
Armaf S.A., 54 Ru du Vertbois, Liege, Belgium	Barrels for double-barrel shotguns
Atlas Arms Inc., 2704 N. Central, Chicago, Ill. 60639	New barrels for double-barrel guns
E. C. Bishop & Son, Inc., Warsaw, Mo. 65355	Stocks and stock blanks
Frederick F. Breitwiser, R.D. # 2, Erin, Ontario Canada	Rifle barrels for shotguns

Brown & Sharp Mfg. Co., Precision Pk. N., Kingston, R.I. 02852	Precision tools
Bob Brownell's, Montezuma, Iowa 50171	General gunsmithing supplies
Browning Arms Co., 1706 Washington St., St. Louis, Mo. 63103	Guns
B-Square Engineering Co., Box 11281, Fort Worth, Texas 76110	Jigs for installing sights & mounts
Maynard Buehler, Orinda, Calif. 94563	Mounts, sights
M. H. Canjar, 500 E. 45th, Denver, Colo. 80216	Triggers
Chicago Wheel & Mfg. Co., 1101 W. Monroe, Chicago, Ill. 60607	Handee grinders, wheels
Christy Gun Works, 875—57th St., Sacramento, Calif. 95831	Pistol & shotgun parts
Coladonato Bros., Box 156, Hazleton, Pa. 18201	Gun cabinets & plans for same
Colt Firearms Co., 150 Huyshope Ave., Hartford, Conn. 06102	Handguns
Dayton-Traister Co., 7028—164 St. S.W., Edmonds, Washington, 98020	Triggers
Dem-Bart Co., 3333 N. Grove St., Tacoma, Wash. 98407	Checkering tools
Dixie Gun Works, Inc., Union City, Tenn. 38261	Antique gun parts
Dumore Co., 1300—17th St., Racine, Wisc. 53403	Hand grinders
Reinhart Fajen, Warsaw, Mo. 65355	Stocks & stock blanks
Firearms International (FN), 4837 Kerby Hill Rd., Washington, D.C. 20022	Guns, foreign
Flaig's Lodge, Millvale, Pa. 15209	Military gun parts
Foredom Electric Co., Rt. 6, Bethel, Conn., 06801	Power grinders
Pete Gould, 1692 N. Dogwood, Coquille, Ore. 97423	Myrtlewood stocks and blanks
Grace Metal Products, Box 67, Elk Rapids, Michigan 49629	Screwdrivers, drifts
Gray's Gun Shop, 2431 Chanticleer, Santa Cruz, California 95060	Gun cabinets
Handy & Harmon, 4140 Gibson Road, El Monte, Calif. 91731	Silver solder & flux

Harrington & Richardson, Park Avenue,   Guns
   Worcester, Mass. 01610
Ithaca Gun Co., Ithaca, N.Y. 14850   Guns
Johnson Gas Appliance Co.,   Gas burners
   Cedar Rapids, Iowa 52401
Iver Johnson Arms & Cycle Works,   Guns
   Fitchburg, Mass. 01420
Lea Mfg. Co., 238 E. Aurora,   Polishing compounds
   Waterbury, Conn. 06720
Bob Lovell, Box 401 Elmhurst, Ill. 60126   Obsolete gun parts
Lyman Gun Sight Corp.,   Sights, mounts, scopes
   Middlefield, Conn. 06455
Marble Arms Co., 1120 Superior,   Sights and scopes
   Gladstone, Mich. 49837
Mashburn Arms Co., 112 W. Sheridan,   Triggers and scope
   Oklahoma City, Oklahoma 73102   mounts
Viggo Miller, 4343 Seward,   Trigger kits
   Omaha, Neb. 68111
Frank Mittermeier, 3577 E. Tremont,   General gunsmith
   N.Y., N.Y. 10465   supplies
Montgomery Ward Gunshop,   Parts, tools
   619 W. Chicago,
   Chicago, Ill. 60610
O. F. Mossberg & Son, Inc.,   Guns
   7 Grasso St.,
   North Haven, Conn. 06473
Numrich Arms,   Obsolete gun parts
   West Hurley, N.Y. 12491
Oakite Products, 19 Rector St.,   Oakite cleaning
   New York 6, N.Y. 10006   compound
Oakley & Merkley, Box 2446,   Stock blanks
   Sacramento, Calif. 95811
Pachmayr Gun Works,   Butt pads
   1220 S. Grand Ave.,
   Los Angeles, Calif. 90015
Robert Patton, Box 13155,   Obsolete Winchester
   San Antonio, Texas 78213   parts
C. R. Pedersen & Son,   Polishing material & gen-
   Ludington, Mich. 49431   eral supplies
Poly-Choke Co., Inc., Box 296,   Chokes
   Hartford, Conn. 06101
Redfield Gunsight Co.,   Sights, mounts &
   5800 E. Jewell Ave.,   telescopes
   Denver, Colo., 80222
Martin B. Retting Inc.,   Gun parts
   11029 Washington,
   Culver City, Calif. 90230

Remington Arms Co.,
   Bridgeport, Conn. 06602

Arms and ammunition

Westley Richards & Co., Ltd.,
   73 Cornwall St.,
   Birmingham 3, England

Barrels for shotguns

Riley's Supply Co., Box 365,
   Avilla, Ind. 46710

Buttplates & caps

Roberts Wood Products, Box 692,
   Olivehurst, Calif. 95961

Stocks & stockblanks

Royal Arms Co.,
   10064 Bert Acosta Ct.,
   Santee, Calif. 92071

Stock blanks

Savage Arms Corp.,
   Westfield, Mass. 01085

Guns

Sears Roebuck, Gun Repair Shop,
   825 St. Louis St.,
   Chicago, Ill. 60607

Tools & parts

Schutzen Gun Works, 1226 Prairie Rd.,
   Colo. Springs, Colo. 80909

Plastic stock finish

Sile Distributors, 7 Center Market Pl.,
   New York, N.Y. 10013

Handgun grips, stocks

Smith & Wesson Inc.,
   Springfield, Mass., 01101

Handguns, rifles

Spokane Sporting Goods, 1718 Sprague,
   Spokane, Wash. 99202

Gun parts

L. S. Starrett Co.,
   Athol, Mass. 01331

Tools

Stoeger Arms Co., 55 Ruta Court,
   S. Hackensack, N.J. 07606

General supplies

Timney Mfg. Co.,
   5624 Imperial Highway,
   South Gate, Calif. 90280

Triggers

Williams Gun Sight Co.,
   7389 Lapeer Rd.,
   Davison, Mich. 48423

Sights, general supplies

Winchester-Western, Products Service
   Department,
   New Haven, Conn. 06504

Guns

W. C. Wolff Co., Box 232,
   Ardmore, Pa. 19003

Springs, parts for old
guns

Index

MORE STACKPOLE BOOKS ON GUNSMITHING AND COLLECTING

CHECKERING AND CARVING OF GUNSTOCKS by Monty Kennedy. The art of gunstock ornamentation is shown in over 470 technical illustrations with full-size patterns ranging from easy to advanced. Eighth printing, 352 pages, 8½ × 11, illustrated. (1952) 0-8117-0630-3. $14.95

FIREARMS BLUEING AND BROWNING by R. H. Angier. A complete manual containing some 230 formulas for both chemical and heat coloring of gun metals. Ninth printing, 160 pages, 5½ × 8¼. (1936) 0-8117-0610-0. $6.95

HOME GUIDE TO MUZZLE LOADERS by George C. Nonte, Jr. Build or restore a muzzle loader; make accessories like powder horns and hunting bags—lore, facts, and how-to advice. Second printing, 224 pages, 8½ × 11 paperback, illustrated. (CIP) (1974) 0-8117-2101-9. $6.95

PISTOLSMITHING by George C. Nonte, Jr. The only book that focuses exclusively on pistols, and repairing them from minor adjustments to complete rebuilding. Fourth printing, 560 pages, 6 × 9, illustrated. (CIP) (1974) 0-8117-1265-6. $14.95

PROFESSIONAL GUNSMITHING by Walter J. Howe. For the firearms tinkerer ready to turn pro—detailed notes on equipping and operating a commercial gunshop and other related topics. Tenth printing, 518 pages, 5¾ × 8⅜, illustrated. (1946) 0-8117-1375-X. $14.95

GUNSMITHING by Roy F. Dunlap. A one-book reference for the gunsmith's shop—tools, supplies, and expert techniques of the trade are featured in detail. Fifth printing, 848 pages, 5¾ × 8½, illustrated. (1963) 0-8117-0770-9. $14.95

GUNSTOCK FINISHING AND CARE by A. Donald Newell. Gives more than 100 formulas for compounding stock finishes, application tips, wood selection, refinishing, stains, plus more. Fifth printing, 5½ × 8¼, illustrated. (1949) 0-8117-0780-6. $12.95

HATCHER'S NOTEBOOK by Gen. Julian S. Hatcher. The standard reference on guns and how they work addresses itself to the complete gunning interests of shooters, gunsmiths, ballisticians, historians, hunters, and collectors. 646 pages, 6 × 9, illustrated. (1962) 0-8117-0795-4. $12.95

SMALL ARMS OF THE WORLD by W. H. B. Smith, revised by E. C. Ezell. The greatest collection of modern weapons ever assembled, disassembled, field-stripped, and loaded in one book answers any question on global firearms design, manufacture, and technology for the arms enthusiast, gun collector, sportsman, or arms technician. Comprehensive coverage is given to the output and weapons-use policies of 42 nations, and precise attention to detail is evident in assembly, disassembly, and maintenance instructions for all major arms. 672 pages, 8½ × 11, index, over 2000 illustrations. (CIP) (1977) 0-8117-1558-2. $20.00